# Adobe InDesign CS2 How-Tos

## 100 Essential Techniques

John Cruise
Kelly Kordes Anton

Adobe Press
ocm 69249105

**Adobe InDesign CS2 How-Tos**
100 Essential Techniques

John Cruise
Kelly Kordes Anton

Adobe Press books are published by Peachpit
Peachpit
1249 Eighth Street
Berkeley, CA 94710
510/524-2178
800/283-9444
510/524-2221 (fax)

For the latest on Adobe Press books, go to www.adobepress.com

Find us on the World Wide Web at: www.peachpit.com

To report errors, please send a note to errata@peachpit.com

Peachpit Press is a division of Pearson Education

Editor: Suzie Nasol
Production Coordinator: Joan Keyes
Copyeditor: Anne Marie Walker
Technical Editor: Laureen Harris
Compositor: Danielle Foster
Indexer: FireCrystal Communications
Cover design: Maureen Forys
Cover production: Owen Wolfson
Interior design: Maureen Forys

ISBN 0-321-32190-1

9 8 7 6 5 4 3 2 1

Printed and bound in the United States of America

# Contents

# CHAPTER ONE

# Getting Started with InDesign

InDesign is a powerful page layout program renowned for its ease of use, precision, and integration with other applications in the Adobe Creative Suite. Hallmark features of InDesign include professional type and graphics handling, drawing tools, transparency, and reliable print and PDF output. With powerful creative tools and flexible workflow features at their fingertips, graphic designers around the globe are using InDesign to produce all types of print and electronic publications. From magazines, books, and newsletters to posters, CD covers, and bumper stickers, many of the publications you see are produced with InDesign—often in concert with Adobe Photoshop and Adobe Illustrator.

InDesign is a mature program with many features. It's possible, after all, to use InDesign to do everything from creating a one-color business card or a five-color magazine to exporting XML tags for an automated catalog system. That's why this book breaks down the software into the 100 most essential tasks you need to know to hit the ground running with InDesign. Whether you're new to page layout software or you're switching from QuarkXPress or PageMaker to InDesign, you can use this book to learn InDesign's most important features and start producing your own high-quality publications.

A few notes about this book may help you understand its approach. Although keyboard shortcuts can really streamline tasks, we did not include them. Almost every feature has a keyboard shortcut, so including them for both Mac OS and Windows adds a significant amount of clutter. For the complete keyboard shortcut list, see the InDesign Help file. In addition, InDesign offers several ways to perform almost every task. Rather than attempt to include every method, we tried to present the easiest and most obvious methods.

In this chapter, you'll learn how to get information about InDesign through the Welcome Screen and Adobe Help Center; customize the software by modifying preferences, keyboard shortcuts, and plug-in sets; and work with InDesign's many palettes.

# #1 Getting Started with the Welcome Screen

When you first launch InDesign, the Welcome screen displays (**Figure 1**). If you're new to InDesign, you can use features of this screen to orient yourself to your new software. If you're ready to launch into a project, however, you can use it to open new and existing files.

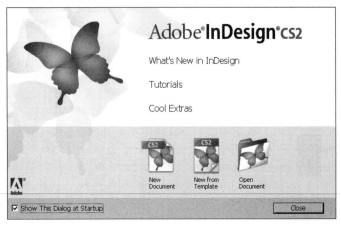

Figure 1 The InDesign Welcome screen provides helpful links and shortcuts.

## Learning About InDesign

To explore InDesign's features and extras, click one of the links at the top of the Welcome screen:

- **What's New in InDesign:** If you have an Internet connection, this takes you to the InDesign section of the Adobe Web site. Click Show Me to see movies of new features in action.

- **Tutorials:** This takes you to the Tutorials section in the Adobe Help Center. You can step through these exercises to familiarize yourself with the software. (It's probably easiest to print them out rather than juggle multiple windows onscreen.)

- **Cool Extras:** This opens a PDF describing the "Cool Extras" provided with InDesign, including templates, sample files, fonts, images, and training resources. Some are automatically installed in your InDesign folder, and you can install others from the installation CDs. (These resources are not included with Educational Packages.)

## Getting to Work

If you're ready to get started on a document, use the buttons at the bottom of the Welcome screen:

- **New Document:** This opens the New Document dialog box so you can set up a new document (see #9 for more information).

- **New Document from Template:** This opens Adobe Bridge so you can locate and open a template to use as the basis for a new document; only use this if you're using Adobe Bridge.

- **Open Document:** This opens the Open a File dialog box to the last location from which InDesign opened a file (see #12 for more information). Click and hold the Open Document button to display a list of recently opened documents.

To bypass the Welcome screen without doing anything, click Close.

**Skipping the Welcome Screen**

If you never use the Welcome screen, you don't have to display it. Uncheck Show This Dialog at Startup in the lower-left corner, and the screen won't display when you launch InDesign. If you change your mind, click Reset All Warning Dialogs in the General panel in the Preferences dialog box.

# #2 Modifying Preferences

Preferences let you customize various features in InDesign—for example, you can change the measurement system, the color of guides, and the display quality. If you're working on a document or project and find yourself thinking "I wish InDesign did it *this* way..." chances are you'll find a preference to fulfill your wish.

The most important aspect to know about preferences is when you're changing them for an individual document and when you're changing them for InDesign:

- When no documents are open, changes to preferences affect all new documents; they do not affect existing documents.

- When documents are open, changes to preferences affect only the active document.

To edit preferences, choose InDesign > Preferences > General (Mac OS) or Edit > Preferences > General (Windows). In the Preferences dialog box (**Figure 2**), click an option in the list at left to display that panel of controls. You can also choose an option from the Preferences submenu (Type, Grids, Spelling, etc.) to open the Preferences dialog box to a specific panel.

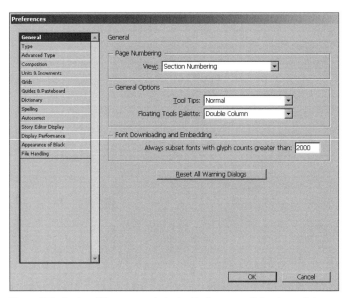

**Figure 2** To display different panels in the Preferences dialog box, click an option in the list at left.

With its 14 panels and almost 100 options, the InDesign Preferences dialog box offers more controls than we can cover in this book. However, if a preference setting has a significant impact on how something works, we bring it up in the context of that feature. For example, we discuss Spelling preferences in #31. It's definitely worth your time to flip through the panels in the Preferences dialog box to see if there's anything you'd like to change. For example, if you're more comfortable working in inches rather than picas, change the default measurement system to inches in the Units & Increments panel.

**Resetting Preferences**

When you're new to a program such as InDesign, it's often best to start out with the default settings. If you inherit a copy of InDesign from another user, you may want to clear out all his or her changes to preferences. To do this, press the following keys while you start up InDesign: Command+Option+Control+Shift (Mac OS) or Ctrl+Alt+Shift (Windows). When the alert asks if you want to delete the preference files, click Yes. Note that this deletes all default settings (such as the text defaults discussed in #27) as well.

# #3 Customizing Keyboard Shortcuts

InDesign provides literally hundreds of keyboard shortcuts to streamline your work. The shortcuts do you little good, however, if you can't remember them. Fortunately, you can change the keyboard shortcuts to better suit the type of work you do and your manual dexterity. For example, if you frequently use the Change Case commands or the Insert Placeholder Text command in the Type menu, you can create keyboard shortcuts for those commands. Or, if a command you use frequently has a finger-contorting shortcut, you can replace it with an easier one.

InDesign stores keyboard shortcuts in sets. You can create your own sets of keyboard shortcuts and select a different set at any time while you're working.

## Selecting a Shortcut Set

To specify a shortcut set to use, choose Edit > Keyboard Shortcuts. Choose an option from the Set menu. If you're switching to InDesign from QuarkXPress 4 or PageMaker 7, you can use that program's keyboard shortcuts for similar features. The selected shortcut set is in use for your copy of InDesign—it is not saved with the active document.

## Editing Shortcut Sets

You can edit the shortcuts for any command in any set—even the Default, QuarkXPress 4 and PageMaker 7 sets. However, it's a good idea to keep these default sets intact. Instead of editing them, create a new set based on one of them, and then edit it. To edit shortcut sets:

1. Choose Edit > Keyboard Shortcuts.

2. Click New Set. Enter a name for the set and choose an option from the Based on Set menu to specify a source for the initial list of keyboard shortcuts. You can also choose an existing set from the Set menu to edit.

3. To locate the command whose shortcut you want to edit, choose an option from the Product Area menu. For example, if the command is in the Type menu, choose Type Menu.

4. Scroll through the Commands list to locate the individual command and select it. For example, if you want to edit the Show Hidden Characters shortcut, select it (**Figure 3**).

5. If the command already has a keyboard shortcut, it's displayed in the Current Shortcuts field. Select it and then click Remove.

6. Click in the New Shortcut field, and press the new keyboard shortcut you'd like to use for the command. A note under the field lets you know if that shortcut is already in use.

7. If you want the shortcut to only work in certain situations—such as when working with text—choose an option from the Context menu. (Otherwise, leave it at Default.)

8. Click Assign.

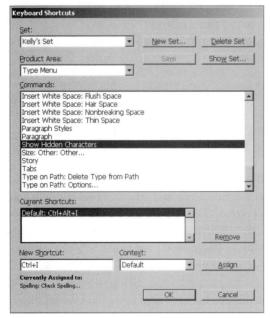

**Figure 3** The Keyboard Shortcuts dialog box lets you select a set of shortcuts to use, create new shortcut sets, and edit the shortcuts for individual commands.

While you're working in the Keyboard Shortcuts dialog box, you can click Save at any time to preserve your changes.

#3: Customizing Keyboard Shortcuts

**Printing Shortcut Sets**

If you want to print out a list of shortcuts for the selected set, click Show Set. A list of commands and their shortcuts displays as a text file in a text-editing window. You can save or print this information.

# #4 Introducing the Toolbox

Ninety-nine percent of the time you're working, you will have the toolbox open so you can create and modify the objects that make up your pages. You'll reach for the toolbox frequently to switch tools, so you'll want to position it and configure it in a way that's convenient for you.

## Positioning the Toolbox

If the toolbox isn't displayed onscreen, choose Window > Tools. To configure and position the toolbox:

- Drag the title bar (the gray bar) at the top or left side of the toolbox to reposition it.

- Double-click the title bar to switch from a double column of tools to a single column or to a single row (**Figure 4a**).

You can also configure the toolbox by choosing an option from the Floating Tools Palette menu in the General panel in the Preferences dialog box. The options are Single Column, Double Column, and Single Row.

**Figure 4a** Double-click the toolbox's title bar to change its configuration from double column to single column to single row.

## Identifying Tools

The toolbox is divided into sections outlined by light gray bars. From top to bottom, the sections are selection tools, drawing and type tools, transformation tools, and modification/navigation tools. If you move the pointer over a tool, a Tool Tip displays the name of the tool and its keyboard shortcut (**Figure 4b**).

If Tool Tips are not displaying, choose Normal or Fast from the Tool Tips menu in the General panel in the Preferences dialog box.

**Setting Tool Preferences**

Some of the object creation tools have preferences that control how they work in the active document. To modify a tool's preferences, double-click the tool and make changes in the dialog box that displays. For example, double-clicking the Type on a Path tool displays the Type on a Path Options dialog box.

**Figure 4b** Point at each tool with the mouse to display a Tool Tip, which tells you the name of the tool and its keyboard shortcut.

## Selecting Tools

To select a tool, move the pointer over it and click it. To use a tool that's hidden in a pop-out menu (indicated by a small triangle next to the tool's icon), click and hold on the tool. When the pop-out menu displays, select another tool (**Figure 4c**). The hidden tool replaces the original tool in the toolbox.

To quickly switch tools, you can press the keyboard shortcut shown in each tool's Tool Tip. For example, you can press "P" to select the Pen tool or "H" to select the Hand tool. (If the text cursor is flashing, you cannot use the single-letter shortcuts.)

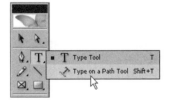

**Figure 4c** To display and select hidden tools, click and hold on a tool's icon.

Some of the options in the toolbox are actually buttons. For example, the butterfly at the top takes you directly to the Adobe Web site, and the buttons at the bottom toggle between Normal and Preview modes.

#4: Introducing the Toolbox

# #5 Using the Control Palette

The context-sensitive Control palette provides comprehensive options for editing whatever is currently selected—a graphics frame, text frame, text, table cells, and more. In fact, if you keep the Control palette open, you are unlikely to need many of InDesign's other palettes and dialog boxes. If you're a QuarkXPress user, you'll immediately recognize the Control palette's similarities with the Measurements palette.

Since the Control palette is so useful, you'll want to keep it handy.

- When you first launch InDesign, the Control palette is docked at the top of the window. (A palette is "docked" when it snaps, or automatically aligns, with the edge of the window.)

- You can drag the Control palette to any location, including docking it to the bottom of the screen, by dragging its title bar (the vertical gray bar at the far left edge of the palette).

- Click the arrow ⊙ at the right side of the Control palette to display a palette menu. At the bottom, you can choose Dock at Top, Dock at Bottom, or Float to position the palette.

- To open and close the Control palette, choose Window > Control.

The Control palette (**Figures 5a–5d**) contains a variety of different panels that are specific to whatever you're editing. The panels switch automatically—for example, if you select a frame using the Selection tool, the Frame panel displays. The only time you have to make a choice is when you're formatting text: You can click the A to display the Character panel or the ¶ to display the Paragraph panel.

As with the toolbox, point the mouse at any control on the Control palette to display its Tool Tip and find out what it does.

**Figure 5a** When text is selected, the Control palette displays either the Character or Paragraph panel. The Character panel lets you choose a font, size, leading, and other formats for highlighted characters.

**Figure 5b** The Paragraph panel provides controls over alignment, indents, space between paragraphs, hyphenation, and more.

**Figure 5c** When a text frame is selected, the Control palette lets you move it, resize it, rotate it, and change the number of columns.

**Figure 5d** When a frame containing a graphic is selected, you can scale the graphic, automatically position it within the frame, and more.

## Quick Access to Even More Power

While the Control palette provides an impressive array of options, it doesn't do everything. For even more control over what you're editing, you can:

- Click the arrow at right to display the palette menu. For example, when the Paragraph panel is displayed, the palette menu provides Hyphenation, Justification, and Paragraph Rules commands.

- Option-click (Mac OS) or Ctrl-click (Windows) icons on the Control palette to open any associated dialog boxes. For example, clicking the Number of Columns icon on the Paragraph panel opens the Text Frame Options dialog box so you can edit anything to do with columns.

- Click the Toggle Palettes button at the far right of the Control palette. This will open related palettes—for example, when the Character panel is displayed, clicking this opens the Character palette and the Character Styles palette.

# #6 Managing Palettes

Like an artist's paint palette, the palettes in InDesign put all the artistic tools you need at your fingertips. However, InDesign offers much more than a Colors palette, resulting in literally scores of palettes that can clutter your screen. If you have a second monitor, you can relocate them there, leaving them open and ready to use. But if you don't have that luxury, particularly if you're working on a laptop or you're using a small monitor, you'll need to control which palettes are open and their position onscreen.

Fortunately, the palettes and the configuration of palettes onscreen are easy to customize. You can even save palette configurations as *workspaces*.

## Palette Basics

To help with palette management, many palettes are combined into *tabbed palette groups*. When palettes are combined into a group, they are said to be *docked*. In addition, palettes can be *collapsed* into a vertical bar on the right side of the screen. The palette configuration is flexible, so you can easily open and manage the palettes you use the most.

- **To open a palette**, choose its name from the Window menu. A quick look at the Window menu gives you an idea of the power in InDesign's palettes: Pages, Colors, Text Wrap, Tables, Layers, and much more.

- **To close a palette**, click its close box or choose its name from the Window menu again.

- **To display a palette within a tabbed group**, click its tab.

- **To create a single palette from a palette in a group**, drag its tab out of the group (**Figure 6a**).

- **To reconfigure a palette group**, drag a tab into a different palette group.

- **To resize a palette**, drag the lower-right corner.

Note that some palettes have keyboard shortcuts—displayed in the Window menu—that open and close them. If you find yourself opening and closing the same palettes, memorize that palette's keyboard shortcut or create one for it (for more information, see #3).

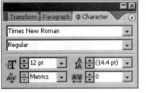

Figure 6a Drag a palette's tab out of the group to create an individual palette for it.

## Collapsing Palettes

Some palettes are collapsed into a vertical bar on the right side of the screen. Click the gray bar to display those palettes (**Figure 6b**). As with other palette groups, you can drag the tabs into their own palettes or into other palette groups. To collapse the palettes again, click the gray bar again.

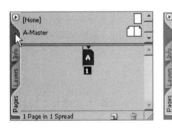

Figure 6b Click the gray bar at left to collapse palettes into a vertical bar on the right side of the InDesign application window.

### Saving a Palette Configuration

Each time you quit InDesign, your current palette configuration is saved—including which palettes are open, their size, how they are grouped, and their locations. The palettes will open in this same way the next time you launch InDesign. If you use certain palette configurations for specific projects, you can save the configuration as a workspace. To do this, set up the palettes the way you want, and then choose Window > Workspace > Save Workspace. Enter a name that indicates the purpose of the configuration—for example, Text Editing or Production. You can then choose that configuration from the Window > Workspace submenu anytime you need those palettes.

# #7 Configuring Plug-ins

Plug-ins are software modules that add features to InDesign. Many basic features of InDesign are actually implemented through plug-ins, so they can be easily updated. You can install additional plug-ins from Adobe and other companies to customize InDesign to your workflow. For example, you might purchase a plug-in that adds sophisticated database publishing features for automatically laying out a catalog.

Adobe makes it easy to find third-party plug-ins to solve your publishing needs, and InDesign makes it easy to control which ones you're using at any given time. Features added by plug-ins are integrated directly into the software as menu commands, palettes, dialog boxes, and so on.

## Finding and Installing Plug-ins

If you have a specific publishing need, check the Adobe Web site (www.adobe.com) for a complete list of plug-ins available for InDesign. If you know that you could save a lot of time if InDesign "just did this," check for a plug-in. You'll find plug-ins for automatically activating fonts as you open documents, for performing math equations in InDesign, and for creating bar codes among the many other plug-ins available.

Once you acquire a plug-in, follow the instructions provided with it for installation. If no instructions are provided, drag the file to the Plug-Ins folder within your InDesign application folder.

## Configuring Plug-ins

If you buy a lot of plug-ins, you'll be tempted to just run them all, all the time. Why get them if you're not going to use them? However, since plug-ins take time to load when you start up InDesign and they sometimes conflict with each other, you might not want to run them all the time. To control which plug-ins load, you can create sets of plug-ins, which you can share with other users. (The plug-ins provided by Adobe in InDesign, however, are required to run and you can't change that.)

To configure the plug-ins running in InDesign, choose InDesign > Configure Plug-ins (Mac OS) or Help > Configure Plug-ins (Windows). In the Configure Plug-ins dialog box (**Figure 7**), you can manage all your plug-ins:

- **Set menu:** Choose a set of plug-ins to edit or to run with InDesign. You cannot edit the default sets (All Plug-ins, Adobe Plug-ins, or Required Plug-ins), but you can duplicate those sets and then edit the duplicates.

- **Plug-ins list:** Click a checkmark to the left of a plug-in name to control whether it loads with InDesign.

- **Duplicate and Rename buttons:** To create a custom set of plug-ins, duplicate one of the default sets and then rename it. For example, you might create a set of plug-ins specifically for production processes.

- **Delete button:** If you no longer need a set of plug-ins, you can remove it by clicking Delete. This does not delete your plug-ins—only the set.

- **Import/Export buttons:** Use these buttons to share plug-in sets in a workgroup; each user needs his or her own copies of the plug-in software as well.

Note that changes in the Configure Plug-ins dialog box—including selecting a new set of plug-ins to load—take effect only when you restart InDesign.

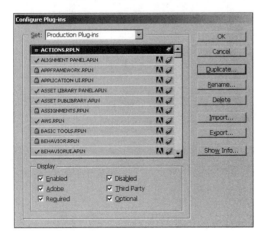

**Figure 7**
The Configure Plug-ins dialog box lets you create custom sets of plug-ins for specific workflows, projects, or clients. Information in this dialog box also helps with troubleshooting.

# #8 Introducing the Adobe Help Center

If you have questions about any feature or process in InDesign—and it's beyond the scope of this book—look no further than the Help menu. Choose InDesign Help from the Help menu to open the comprehensive Adobe Help Center (**Figure 8**). The Help Center actually provides more information than any printed documentation you receive from Adobe. It's also your best first move in terms of troubleshooting.

Depending on the speed of your computer, the Help Center may take a little time to load. Therefore, you may prefer to keep its window open but behind other windows. If the window size is overwhelming—for example, if you want to see the page you're working on and the help at the same time—you can shrink the window. Click the Compact View button in the upper-right corner to condense the window so it displays only the text of the current topic along with Previous Topic, Next Topic, and history buttons.

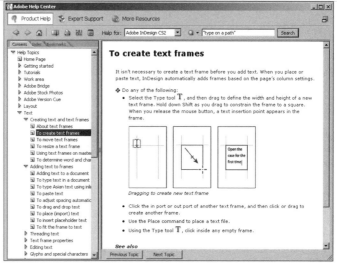

**Figure 8** The Adobe Help Center provides comprehensive documentation and resources for all installed Adobe products.

## Taking a Tour

At the top of the Help Center, you can click a button to specify what you're looking for:

- **Product Help** displays help for all installed Adobe products; you can choose a product from the Help For menu.

- **Export Support** describes the technical support plans available from Adobe.

- **More Resources** provides links to online resources, including Support, Tips and Tutorials, Forms, and Training.

You'll be in the Product Help window most of the time, which provides a navigation area at left (Contents, Index, and Bookmarks) and displays the actual help text at right. The second row of buttons lets you navigate and print help topics; as with other buttons in InDesign, point at them with the mouse to display their Tool Tips.

## Searching the Help

To locate information, you can scroll through the Contents list, double-clicking topics to display subtopics or text. This works well if you need a full overview of a topic, such as "Color." If you need a quick answer, however, try the Search field in the upper-right corner. Searching works well for finding out what a specific command does or how to complete a specific task. Here are a few tips for searching:

- To find out how to do something, use "to" in your search text. For example, type "To create a text path" rather than "creating text paths."

- Put quotation marks around specific phrases to locate them. For example, if you want to find out what the Save Workspace command does, enter "save workspace" with quotation marks. This produces two results, one of them called "To customize the workspace." Entering the same phrase without quotation marks produces about 50 results for you to wade through.

- If you've installed the entire Adobe Creative Suite, the help file often includes information about Adobe Bridge. If you're not using Adobe Bridge, it's safe to ignore this information and focus on information about InDesign only.

#8: Introducing the Adobe Help Center

---

**Updating the Help**

If you have an Internet connection, you can update the help file at any time. Click the Preferences button [⊞] in the Adobe Help Center and then click Check for Updates. This notifies you about application and help file updates for all installed Adobe products.

# CHAPTER TWO

# Working with Documents

In InDesign, a document is an individual file that contains the layout for a publication—an advertisement, brochure, newsletter, book chapter, or magazine article, for example. When you create a document, you specify fundamental aspects of the publication, such as the page size, margins, and number of columns. These settings can be saved as document presets so you can quickly and consistently create documents with the same settings.

In this chapter you'll learn to create, open, close, save, and navigate documents. Once you create a document, you enter the workspace known as the document window. The window displays the pages of your publication along with a variety of layout and navigational aids. Within the window, InDesign provides convenient options for navigating through pages, changing the view scale, and previewing the output. For ease in file management, InDesign allows you to save metadata such as keywords and creator names with documents. You'll learn to work within the document window, change the view, preview output, and save metadata as well.

# #9 Creating New Documents

When you start a new project—such as a newsletter—you create a new document that reflects the finished page size, margins, and number of columns. In addition, you can specify the number of pages and whether the document has facing pages (as in a book). As a starting place, it may be helpful to mock up your publication first, even just by roughing it out with pen and paper. While all these options can be changed after you create the document, the layout will be easier if you know the specifics up front.

To create a new document:

1. Choose File > New > Document. The New Document dialog box (**Figure 9**) lets you set up the document.

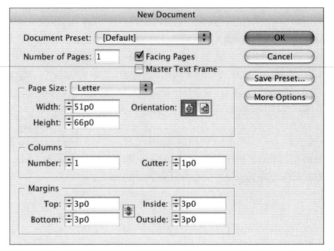

**Figure 9** The New Document dialog box lets you specify the number of pages, page size, margins, and more for a new project.

2. Enter a value in the Number of Pages field. You can create documents with up to 9,999 pages.

3. To create a document with two-page spreads as in a book or magazine, check Facing Pages.

4. To automatically place a text frame—a container for text—on the pages, check Master Text Frame. The master text frame will be placed according to the values in the Columns and Margins areas.

5. Choose an option from the Page Size menu or enter values in the Width and Height fields. To quickly reverse the Width and Height values, click the Orientation buttons.

6. In the Columns area, enter the number of columns most of the pages will have in the Number field. Enter the amount of space you want between columns in the Gutter field.

7. In the Margins area, enter values in the Top, Bottom, Left, and Right fields to specify margin guides for the pages. If you check Facing Pages, the Left and Right fields change to Inside and Outside. If you want all the margin values to be the same, click the Make All Settings the Same button ▒ between the fields.

8. Click OK to create the new document.

InDesign creates a new document with the number of pages you specified. Magenta-colored guides on the page indicate margins and violet-colored guides indicate columns. If you checked Master Text Frame, a text frame (a container for text) is automatically placed within the margin guides, and contains the number of columns you specified. Your designs, however, are not constrained by anything you specify for the new document. For example, you can add and remove pages, change the number of columns in any or all of the text frames, and work with the entire page area regardless of the margins.

## Entering Values in Different Measurement Systems

The default measurement system for new documents is picas, which are commonly used in graphic design. (A pica is approximately one-sixth of an inch or 12 points.) You can enter values in any measurement system as long as you include an abbreviation with the values—for example, "in" for inches or "pt" for points. The abbreviations for the supported measurement systems are

- Inches: i, in, inch, or "
- Millimeters: mm
- Picas: p
- Points: pt (or "p" before the value)
- Picas and points: p (after the pica value, before the point value)
- Ciceros: c

# #10 Saving Document Presets

If you find yourself in the tedious situation of setting up similar documents over and over—for example, if you create new trifold brochures several times a week—you can save all the settings in the New Document dialog box as *document presets*. You can then select from your document presets in the New Document dialog box. This not only saves you time when creating new documents, but it ensures consistency among similar documents. Never again will you wonder about the page size for the book jackets you're working on or the bleed area for a magazine.

## Saving Document Presets

To save document presets:

1. Choose File > New > Document. In the New Document dialog box, specify the Number of Pages, Page Size, Columns, Margins, and all other attributes you want in the preset.

2. Click Save Preset. In the Save Preset dialog box (**Figure 10a**), type a name for the document preset in the field.

3. Click OK. The new document preset is saved with your copy of InDesign.

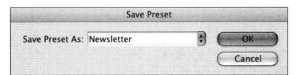

Figure 10a The Save Preset dialog box lets you name and save all the specifications for a new document.

## Using Document Presets

To use a document preset, select it from the Document Preset menu (**Figure 10b**) at the top of the New Document dialog box. All the settings in the dialog box automatically change to those in the preset. You can also choose one of your presets from the Document Preset submenu in the File menu; this automatically opens the New Document dialog box with the preset selected.

**Note**

*If you select a document preset, and then make further changes in the New Document dialog box, the Document Preset menu lets you know by changing to [Custom].*

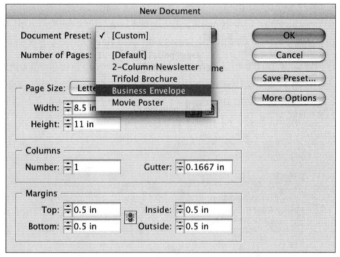

**Figure 10b** The Document Preset menu in the New Document dialog box lets you create new documents quickly and efficiently by choosing from your custom list of document setups.

## Editing Document Presets

In addition to creating a document preset using the New Document dialog box, you can also use the Document Presets dialog box (**Figure 10c**) to create a preset. To open this dialog box, choose File > Document Presets > Define. The dialog box works as follows:

- **Presets list:** The Presets list shows all your document presets. Click one to see its settings, edit it, or delete it.

- **Preset Settings area:** This scroll box shows all the document specifications for the selected document preset.

*(continued on next page)*

- **New button:** Click New to set up a new document preset; a version of the New Document dialog box displays so you can name and set up the preset.

- **Edit button:** Click Edit to change the name or specifications of the selected document preset.

- **Delete button:** Click Delete to remove the selected document presets from the list; you cannot delete Default.

- **Load button:** Click Load to add document presets from another InDesign user to your list. (In the Load Document Presets dialog box, a document presets file will have a .dcst extension.)

- **Save button:** Click Save to export selected document presets to share with another user. Within a workgroup, it's a good idea to share presets so you can ensure the same specifications for similar projects.

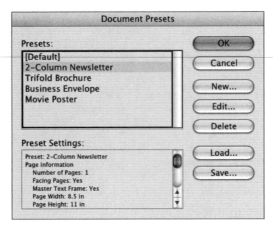

**Figure 10c** The Document Presets dialog box lets you create, edit, and delete document presets and share document presets with other users.

# #11 Understanding the Document Window

The document window is the space you work within for each InDesign document. The document window mimics an actual paste-up board with a blank area surrounding pages called the *pasteboard* and layout aids such as rulers, guides, and grids. Within each document window, you can control the view scale, the quality of the display, and which layout aids are showing. Most of the time, the document window displays the page or spread you are currently working on. Since it may be helpful to see different pages of a document at the same time (or different view scales), you can open multiple windows for the same open document.

## Reviewing the Document Window

Take a look at a standard document window (**Figure 11a**).

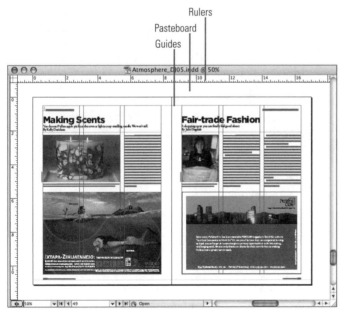

**Figure 11a** The document window provides a work space similar to a traditional paste-up board.

You can customize many aspects of the document window using the Preferences dialog box. For example, if you prefer to work in inches rather than points or you can't stand magenta guides, you can change those settings. The Units & Increments panel lets you specify the increments for the rulers and the Guides & Pasteboard panel lets you change guide colors and modify the pasteboard.

- Rulers appear along the top and left side of the document window. The View > Show/Hide Rulers command lets you control whether or not the rulers display.

- A white pasteboard surrounds each page or spread. Each page or spread has its own pasteboard, which you can use for temporarily storing objects or for creating and formatting objects away from the distractions of the page.

- Different colored guides and grids may display on the pages depending on the settings in the View > Grids & Guides submenu. Generally, you will see magenta margin guides and violet column guides.

## Navigating Documents

The lower-left corner of the document window provides convenient controls for displaying file information and navigating documents (**Figure 11b**).

- The Show Structure arrow in the left corner lets you display the Structure panel for working with XML content.

- The View Percent controls, to the right of the Show Structure arrow, let you change the view scale (see #16 for more information).

- The Page Number controls, to the right of the View Percent controls, lets you choose the page or spread to display (see #15 for more information).

- The Open area displays the status of the active document. For an Open document, point at this area to display the full path to the file.

- Standard scroll bars let you move around within a document.

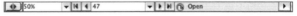

**Figure 11b** The lower-left corner contains controls for changing the view percent and selecting pages to display.

If you are working on a document and want to see different view of it—for example, to view the first and last page at the same time or view the same page at 50 percent and 300 percent—you can open another window for the document. Simply choose Window > Arrange > New Window.

Once you have multiple windows open, whether of a single document or multiple documents, you create a management issue. The bottom of the Window menu lists all the open document windows so you can choose one to display. Commands in the Window > Arrange submenu also help you manage document windows:

- **Cascade:** Choose Window > Arrange > Cascade to overlap the document windows slightly so you can see the title bar of each.

- **Tile:** Choose Window > Arrange > Tile to resize and arrange the document windows as necessary so you can see all of each window.

- **Minimize:** Choose Window > Arrange > Minimize to hide the active document window in the Mac OS X dock or the Windows taskbar.

**Closing Document Windows**

To close a document and all its open windows, press Command+Shift+W (Mac OS) or Ctrl+Shift+W (Windows). To close all open documents and their windows, add the Option/Alt key: Command+Option+Shift+W (Mac OS) or Ctrl+Alt+Shift+W (Windows).

# #12 Opening Documents

It's easy to open files in InDesign—it's just like opening files in other applications. You are, however, likely to encounter some confusing alerts that you might not be sure how to handle. These alerts may warn you about missing fonts and missing graphic files—external files that may be required to output the document correctly. Sometimes, you can safely bypass these alerts, but other times you really need to pay attention to them.

To open documents:

1. Choose File > Open.

2. Locate and select the InDesign documents you want to open. You can select multiple documents by Command-clicking (Mac OS) or Ctrl-clicking (Windows) the files; Shift-click to select a continuous range of files.

3. At the bottom of the Open a File dialog box (**Figure 12a**), click Open Normal to simply open the selected documents or copies of selected templates.

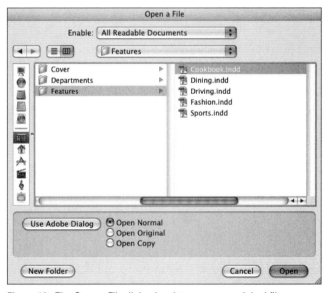

**Figure 12a** The Open a File dialog box lets you open original files or copies of files.

*Tip*

*You can also click Open Original to open a template (rather than a copy of it). Click Open Copy to open a new, unnamed copy of selected documents or templates.*

**4.** Click Open.

## Handling Missing Fonts

If the document uses fonts that are not active on your system, the Missing Fonts dialog box (**Figure 12b**) lists those fonts. The best way to handle this problem is to use your font management application—such as FontBook, Suitcase, or Suitcase Fusion—to activate the fonts listed. Your other option is to click Find Font to display the Find Font dialog box, which lets you replace missing fonts with active fonts and locate font files on your computer. Keep in mind that replacing missing fonts with different fonts can alter the design and reflow all the text. You can also bypass the Missing Fonts dialog box by clicking OK. InDesign will temporarily substitute a system font until you activate the appropriate fonts.

**Shortcuts for Opening Files**

As with other applications, you can open an InDesign document by double-clicking its file icon on your desktop. If InDesign is not running, double-clicking a document launches the latest version of InDesign on your computer. You can also drag InDesign file icons on top of the InDesign application icon.

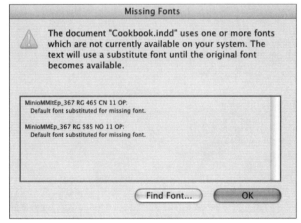

**Figure 12b** The Missing Fonts dialog box lists fonts used in the document that are not active on your system.

## Fixing Graphic Links

When you import graphics into InDesign documents, it keeps track of the location of those graphic files and the last edited dates of those graphics. If you change or move the graphic files, InDesign notifies you when you open the document. If an alert reports Missing Links or Modified Links when you open a document, you can click Fix Links Automatically to find and update the graphic files. As with fonts, you need the original graphic files to be available for proper output. If, however, you're simply opening the document to edit text, you do not need to worry about the links. In that case, click Don't Fix. You can always update the links later using the Links palette (Window menu).

# #**13** Saving Documents and Templates

InDesign automatically saves your work and recovers it even if the program unexpectedly quits. Nonetheless, once you create a new document, it's a good idea to name and save it so you know where the file is and what it's called. If you're designing a *template*—a pre-designed starting place for a new project—you can save a document as a template. A template opens as a new, unsaved document.

## Saving Documents

To save the active document:

- To save a new, unnamed document, choose File > Save or File > Save As. Use the Save As dialog box to specify a name and location for the file.

- To save a copy of the document, choose File > Save a Copy. Use the Save a Copy dialog box to specify a different name or location for the file. The active document remains open; you will need to open the copy to work on it.

- To save your work in progress, choose File > Save at any time. Unlike some other applications, however, InDesign does not require you to obsessively save your work. Changes are automatically saved to a temporary file with the extension .idlk, which is created in the same location where the document is saved. If InDesign crashes, changes are restored from this temporary file automatically.

## Creating Templates

A template is a document that serves as the "shell" for a new publication, so it should be as complete as possible. Start by reviewing the document to make sure it includes everything you might need in a template—master pages (preformatted pages), paragraph and character styles (for formatting text), page guides (for positioning objects), colors, and more.

## InDesign File Extensions

When working with InDesign, file extensions help you identify the primary file types:

- .indd for documents
- .indt for templates
- .indl for libraries (for storing objects)
- .indb for books (for managing multiple documents)

To create a template:

1. Save the document and then choose File > Save As.

2. In the Save As dialog box (**Figure 13**), choose InDesign CS2 template from the Format menu (Mac OS) or Save As Type menu (Windows).

3. Specify a location for the file. If the template is for a workgroup, you might store it on a shared server.

4. Type a name for the template in the Save As field. To identify the file as a template, InDesign adds the file extension .indt.

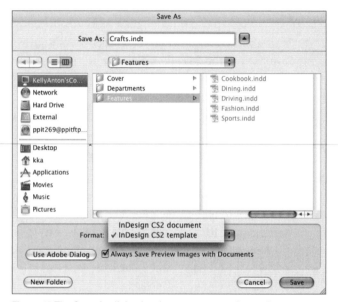

**Figure 13** The Save As dialog box lets you name and save documents and templates.

# #14 Adding Metadata to Documents

*Metadata* is information stored with a file that helps you track who created it, what it's for, and what's in it. Metadata is particularly useful as search criteria when using Adobe Bridge to manage files—for example, you can save keywords with documents and then search for documents containing those keywords. While metadata can be extremely detailed and powerful, you can customize it to your workflow so you're only storing the metadata you actually need. For example, you can limit your use of metadata to simply saving the name of a file's creator with it. Or, you can extend the use of metadata to include copyright information, keywords, details about the source of imported text and graphic files, and much more.

To store metadata with the active document, choose File > File Info. Use the File Info dialog box (**Figure 14**) to save categories of information with the document. In the Description panel, you can fill in any of the fields that might be helpful to you in locating the document or tracking its information.

- **Document Title, Author, Author Title:** In these fields, you might type information such as the name of the file, the name of the person who created it, and the person's job title. Or, you might type an article headline, the writer's name, and the writer's affiliation.

- **Description and Description Writer:** Type a description of what the file contains and the name of the person who wrote the description.

- **Keywords:** Type keywords to associate with the document when searching for it. Separate multiple keywords with commas.

- **Copyright Status, Copyright Notice, Copyright Info URL:** If you want to store copyright information with a document, you can choose Copyrighted from the Copyright Status menu. If available, type or paste the Copyright Notice in the field or click Go to URL to link to the notice. If you know the information is not copyrighted, you can choose Public Domain from the menu.

## Metadata Format

InDesign stores metadata in Extensible Metadata Platform format, or XMP. The XMP format is based on XML and is compatible with Adobe Bridge and all the Adobe Creative Suite applications. This allows you to use the same metadata strategy throughout your creative workflow.

**Tip**

*For consistency, if you have saved information with files before, you can choose that information from menus to the right of the fields. For example, you can choose keywords from a list to make sure you're using the same words each time.*

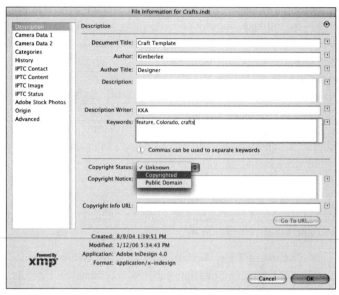

**Figure 14** The Description panel in the File Info dialog box lets you save metadata with a document, including keywords and copyright information.

To display other panels of information in the File Info dialog box, click options in the list at left. The remaining panels let you track the source of imported images and text files, including content from news sources. The Advanced panel lets you import, export, and append metadata.

# #**15** Navigating Documents

InDesign offers many ways to navigate within a page or spread and to jump from page to page—so many in fact that you're unlikely to remember them all. The best thing to do is figure out your favorite way to navigate and then memorize it. If you're a visual person, for example, you may prefer the Navigator palette or the Hand tool. If you're entering edits from hard copy, you may prefer to jump to specific page numbers.

Options for jumping to a specific page number:

- Press Command+J (Mac OS) or Ctrl+J (Windows) to highlight the Page Number field in the document window. Type in the page number and press Return/Enter.

- Click the Page Number field in the document window to display a list of page numbers to choose from (**Figure 15a**).

- Double-click a page icon in the Pages palette (Window menu).

**Figure 15a** The Page Number field/menu in the lower-left corner of the document window makes it easy to jump to a specific page.

## Absolute Page Numbers

When you enter page numbers in fields—such as the Page Number field in the document window—you have the option to enter absolute page numbers. An absolute page number indicates a page's actual position in the document as opposed to the page number assigned using the Numbering & Section Options dialog box (Pages palette menu). To enter an absolute page number, precede it with a plus sign. To jump to the first page of a document, for example, type +1 in the Page Number field.

Options for jumping to different pages and spreads:

- Use the Layout menu commands: First Page, Previous Page, Next Page, Last Page, Next Spread, Previous Spread, Go Back, and Go Forward. The keyboard commands for these options display in the menu (the arrows shown in the commands refer to the Page Up and Page Down keys on your keyboard).

- Use the arrows on either side of the Page Number field in the lower-left corner of the document window (**Figure 15b**). From left to right, the arrows work as follows: First Spread, Previous Spread, Next Spread, and Last Spread.

**Figure 15b** The arrows on either side of the Page Number field/menu let you quickly flip through the spreads in a document.

Options for scrolling:

- Use the scroll bars in the document window. Although this can be an imprecise way of navigating a long document, it may be helpful in locating a spot within a page or spread.

- Select the Hand tool in the toolbox. Click and drag to navigate within a page or between pages and spreads. To use the Hand tool without actually switching tools, press the Spacebar for temporary access to it. If the cursor is blinking in text, press Option (Mac OS) or Alt (Windows) along with the Spacebar.

- Drag the red square on the Navigator palette (Window > Object & Layout > Navigator) to display a specific area on a page or spread. Choose View All Spreads from the palette menu to navigate the entire document (**Figure 15c**). Controls at the bottom of the Navigator palette let you change the document's view scale and the size of the red square in relation to the thumbnails.

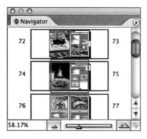

**Figure 15c** The Navigator palette lets you quickly scroll through page previews to find the area you're looking for.

# #16 Viewing Documents

To view anything, from a snapshot of an entire document to the curves of an individual character, InDesign lets you adjust the view scale from 5 percent to 4,000 percent. You can adjust the view scale—often referred to as zooming in or zooming out—using a variety of methods. In addition to changing the view scale, you can control the quality of the display and preview various output options such as bleeds.

## Adjusting the View Scale

Options for adjusting the view scale:

- Press Command+Option+5 (Mac OS) or Ctrl+Alt+5 (Windows) to highlight the Zoom Percent field in the document window. Type in a view scale percentage and press Return/Enter.

- Click the Zoom Percent field in the document window to display a menu of zoom percentages to choose from (**Figure 16a**).

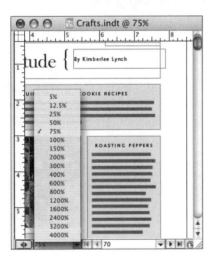

**Figure 16a** The Zoom Percent field/menu in the lower-left corner of the document window lets you type or select a view scale.

- Choose options from the View menu: Zoom In, Zoom Out, Fit Page in Window, Fit Spread in Window, Actual Size, or Entire Pasteboard. The keyboard commands for these options display in the menu—it's worthwhile to memorize those you use the most.

*(continued on next page)*

## Accessing the Zoom Tool

Since you may need to zoom in and out of a document frequently, you can access the Zoom tool without switching tools. Simply press Command+Spacebar (Mac OS) or Ctrl+Spacebar (Windows) to display the Zoom In tool. Add the Option key (Mac OS) or Alt key (Windows) to access the Zoom Out tool.

- Select the Zoom tool 🔍 in the toolbox. Click the Zoom tool on the page to zoom in; each click increases the view scale to the next increment in the Zoom Percent menu (5%, 12.5%, 25%, 50%, 75%, 100%, 150%, etc.). Click and drag to zoom in on a specific area. To zoom out, press the Option key (Mac OS) or Alt key (Windows) while the Zoom tool is selected.

- Use the Zoom Percent field, Zoom In, and Zoom Out controls at the bottom of the Navigator palette (Window > Object & Layout > Navigator).

## Adjusting the Display Quality

If you feel like InDesign is "slow" or what you see onscreen looks "rough," you may need to adjust the display quality. You can customize the quality of the display to make it faster or more detailed. To change the quality, choose an option from the Display Performance submenu in the View menu:

- **Fast Display:** Specifies 24 dpi screen resolution with no transparency; this view is helpful for users with slower computers who may simply be editing text.

- **Typical Display:** Specifies 72 dpi screen resolution with low-resolution transparency display; this view balances speed with quality for most layout work.

- **High Quality Display:** Specifies 144 dpi screen resolution and detailed transparency effects such as drop shadows and feathering; this view is useful for soft proofing—attempting to proof color output onscreen.

You can customize the default display quality in the Display Performance panel in the Preferences dialog box. In addition, if Allow Object Level Display Settings is checked in the Display Performance submenu (View menu), you can customize the display on an object-by-object basis. To do this, select the object and choose Object > Display Performance. You might, for example, specify High Quality for a specific transparency effect so you can view the text behind it.

# Previewing Output

The View menu also provides options for previewing final output:

- **Overprint Preview:** Choose this option to see how spot colors interact with any transparency effects.

- **Proof Setup and Proof Colors:** Use these options when soft proofing. The success of soft proofing depends largely on the quality of your monitor, whether you are using color management (see #78 for more information), and your experience with printing and production processes.

- **Screen Mode:** Use options in the Screen Mode submenu to switch among Normal, Preview, Bleed, and Slug modes. Preview mode hides all nonprinting page elements such as guides and hidden characters so you can see how pages will look when printed. The Bleed and Slug modes both hide nonprinting page elements but show objects in the Bleed or Slug area as defined in the New Document dialog box. You can quickly switch among Screen Modes using the buttons at the bottom of the toolbox (**Figure 16b**).

Figure 16b The Screen Mode buttons at the bottom of the toolbox let you quickly switch among Normal (left) and Preview, Bleed, and Slug (right) modes.

**Actual Size**

To quickly display a document at 100 percent or Actual Size, double-click the Zoom tool in the toolbox. You can also press Command+0 (Mac OS) or Ctrl+0 (Windows).

# CHAPTER THREE

# Working with Text

InDesign can do everything from serving as your primary word processor to importing text from other programs to automatically applying specialized formatting. In InDesign, text is placed inside text frames or it flows along type paths, both of which can be any size or shape. Text frames and type paths can be linked (or *threaded*) to each other to flow text through a document.

When it comes to formatting text, you have a variety of options for applying character and paragraph formats, including *styles* for automated formatting. InDesign also provides expert options for setting tabs and creating bulleted and numbered lists. For word processing, InDesign provides a story editor, spell check features, and search-and-replace functions.

In this chapter you'll learn how to create text frames and type paths, and then how to add, format, and edit text.

# #17 Creating Text Frames

Most of the text you see in an InDesign layout—headlines, articles, figure captions, ad copy—is contained by invisible, rectangular text frames. You can, however, draw text frames of any shape, and you can use the master text frame you specify in the New Document dialog box.

## Drawing Text Frames

To create a rectangular text frame, select the Type tool [T] on the toolbox. Click and drag to draw a text frame. Use the rulers and values in the Control palette to judge the size and placement of the text frame (**Figure 17a**).

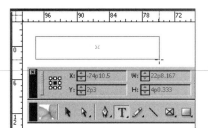

**Figure 17a** While dragging with the Type tool to create a rectangular text frame, you can use the rulers and Control palette to judge its size and placement.

To create a round or variable-shape text frame, use any of the drawing tools to create a frame (see #49 for more information). Then, simply click it with the Type tool to enter text (**Figure 17b**). You can also click any frame using the Selection tool or Direct Selection tool and choose Object > Content > Text to convert it to a text frame.

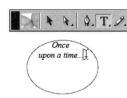

**Figure 17b** To place text in a round text frame, draw an elliptical graphics frame with the Ellipse Frame tool, click it with the Type tool, and then start typing.

## Using the Master Text Frame

If you're importing long blocks of text onto pages—for a book chapter or annual report, for example—you don't have to draw a text frame on each page. You can automatically place a text frame on each document page by checking Master Text Frame in the New Document dialog box (File > New > Document). The values in the Columns and Margins areas control the number of columns in the master text frame, the amount of space between columns, and the placement on the page (**Figure 17c**).

To enter text in the master text frame on document pages, select the Type tool and Command+Shift-click (Mac OS) or Ctrl+Shift-click (Windows) on the text frame.

### Note

*The master text frame is placed on pages that are based on the default master page, A-Master. If you create new master pages, they will contain the master text frame as well (although you can delete it). See #79 for more information about master pages.*

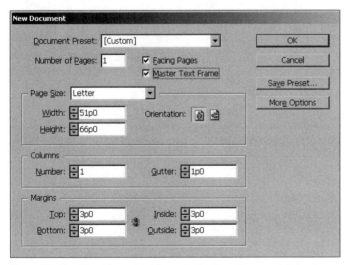

**Figure 17c** Checking Master Text Frame in the New Document dialog box automatically places a text frame on document pages according to the values in the Columns and Margins areas.

### Creating Squares and Circles

To create a square text frame, press the Shift key as you drag the Type tool. This constrains the Type tool to creating text frames with four sides of equal length. Similarly, press the Shift key as you drag the Ellipse Frame tool to create a circle.

# #18 Modifying Text Frames

So what good are text frames, considering that you can't see them? While their primary purpose is to contain text, you can also modify text frames to complement your layout. A magazine article, for example, generally features a rectangular text frame with a stroke around it, two columns of text inset from the edges of the stroke, and possibly a fill (background color). To achieve these effects, you can control the positioning of text within text frames (specifying the number of columns, for example), and you can format text frames like any other object (applying a stroke, fill, and drop shadow, for example). To format text frames, select them with the Type tool, the Selection tool, or the Direct Selection tool.

## Setting Up Columns

To modify the number of columns in a text frame, select the frame and choose Object > Text Frame Options. In the Columns area in the General panel (**Figure 18**) work as follows:

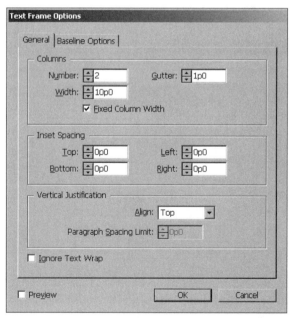

Figure 18 The General panel in the Text Frame Options dialog box lets you specify the position of text within the frame.

1. Enter the number of columns for the text frame in the Number field and the amount of space you want between columns in the Gutter field.

2. If you want the columns to be a specific width, enter a value in the Width field. You don't have to be a math wiz here—if the number of columns, the width, and the gutter you specify won't fit in the text frame, InDesign will automatically adjust the text frame.

3. Check Fixed Column Width to keep the width of the columns the same—even if the text frame is resized. Rather than adjusting column width, InDesign will change the number of columns and the frame will be automatically resized to accommodate the specified column width. For example, say you want to make a two-column text frame a tiny bit wider. If Fixed Column Width is checked, the text frame will automatically become wide enough to hold three columns of the specified width.

## Specifying Text Inset and Vertical Alignment

The General panel in the Text Frame Options dialog box (Object menu) also lets you adjust the amount of space between the edges of a text frame and the text. The need for this value is not apparent, however, until you stroke the edges of a frame or apply a fill to it and realize that the text is touching the edges of the frame. To adjust text inset, type values in the Top, Bottom, Left, and Right fields in the Inset Spacing area.

### Note
*For nonrectangular text frames, such as elliptical text frames, you can only have one inset value.*

For even more control over the placement of text within a frame, you can specify how the text is placed vertically in the General panel in the Text Frame Options dialog box. For example, you can specify that text is centered vertically within the frame—an option that works well for cards, invitations, ads, and so on.

**Changing Columns and Vertical Alignment**

The Control palette provides a quick method for changing the number of columns in a frame and for experimenting with different vertical justification options. When a text frame is selected using the Selection tool or the Direct Selection tool, the far right side of the Control palette provides a Number of Columns field and vertical alignment buttons. If you're not sure what the controls do, point at them with the mouse to display their Tool Tips.

## Formatting Text Frames

To see a text frame in a layout, you can apply a stroke to its edges, apply a fill or gradient, add a drop shadow, and more. For more information, see #60, #61, and #64.

## Using the Baseline Grid

A baseline grid consists of horizontal lines that text "sits" on. Setting up a baseline grid for an entire document or an individual text frame makes it easy to align text horizontally across columns regardless of varying leading and spacing values before and after paragraphs. Generally, the distance specified between gridlines in the baseline grid is the same as the leading value for body text (around 12 points, for example). Some graphic designers swear by the baseline grid for carefully positioning text, whereas others sneer at its use, likening it to a paint-by-the-numbers painting.

You can set up a baseline grid for a document in the Grids panel in the Preferences dialog box. In addition, individual text frames can have their own grids set up in the Baseline Options panel in the Text Frame Options dialog box (Object menu). Once you set up a baseline grid, you still need to "snap" paragraphs to it by selecting them and clicking Align to Baseline Grid in the Paragraph palette or Control palette. The View > Grids & Guides submenu lets you show and hide the baseline grid.

# #**19** Threading Text Frames

Right away you'll notice that all your text doesn't always fit into one frame. Plus, you may not want all your text crammed into a single frame. To solve this dilemma, InDesign lets you link text frames to each other through a process called *threading*. When text frames are threaded, one long block of text—such as a newspaper story or a series of one-paragraph catalog descriptions—flows from one frame to the next.

All the text within a series of threaded frames is referred to as a *story*. Working with a story—as opposed to multiple unthreaded text frames containing text—has many advantages. You can edit stories in the Story Editor; limit a spell check or search-and-replace function to only the text in a story; or select all the text in a story to reformat it, export it, or copy and paste it. All the advantages of working with stories make threading text frames particularly important.

You can thread two or more empty text frames, and you can thread text frames to an existing frame. You cannot, however, add text frames to a thread if they already contain text. To thread text frames, use the Selection tool or the Direct Selection tool.

## Preparing to Thread

To start threading text frames, you need to be able to see and understand what you're doing. Choose View > Show Frame Edges to see outlines of the text frames. Then, choose View > Show Text Threads so you can see the links between frames. With the Selection tool, click a text frame to identify its *in port* in its upper-left corner and its *out port* in its lower-right corner (**Figure 19a**). To link text frames, you need to click the out ports and in ports.

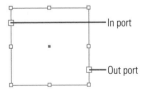

Figure 19a The upper-left corner of each text frame contains an in port (1) and the lower-right corner contains an out port (2).

## Threading Two Frames

To thread text frames, click the out port of the first text frame and then click the in port of the second text frame.

1. To thread two text frames, click the Selection tool or the Direct Selection tool.

2. Click the text frame you want to start threading from—this frame may or may not contain text.

3. Click the text frame's out port in the lower-right corner; the loaded text icon displays.

4. Navigate to the second text frame, even if it's on another page of the document. When the cursor is over the text frame, the thread icon displays.

5. Click the thread icon on the second text frame's in port to thread the two text frames (**Figure 19b**). In addition to clicking an existing text frame, you can also click and drag to create a new text frame that is threaded to the first frame.

6. Notice the line (or thread) between the two text frames (**Figure 19c**). To link additional text frames, repeat this process.

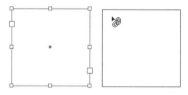

**Figure 19b** To thread text frames, click a text frame's out port using the Selection tool. Then, click another text frame's in port.

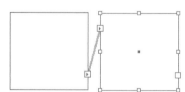

**Figure 19c** A line between two ports indicates threaded text frames.

Threading is not limited to text frames. You can thread type paths to each other, thread a text frame to a type path, and thread a type path to a text frame. For example, you can flow a headline along a type path and then thread to a text frame containing the article.

## Working with Threaded Text Frames

Once you thread text frames, you're not stuck with them—you can add frames within a thread, reroute threads, delete threaded text frames without losing text, and break threads.

- **To insert a text frame** into a series of threaded frames, simply click the out port of the preceding text frame and click in the new text frame.

- **To reroute threads**, click an out port and then click the in port of the frame to which you want to reroute the text.

- **To delete a frame** within a series of threaded text frames, select it and choose Edit > Clear. Text is automatically reflowed into the remaining threaded text frames. Deleting a text frame from a series of threaded frames does not delete the text within the frame. Rather, the text is flowed into the remaining frames.

- **To break a text thread**, double-click an out port or an in port. The thread between the two text frames will be broken, and the text after the broken thread will become overset (see Recognizing Overset Text sidebar).

The master text frame, specified in the New Document dialog box (File > New > Document), is automatically threaded from page to page.

# #20 Creating Type Paths

Text is not restricted to placement inside frames: You can flow text along any shape path, including along a straight line, a curved line, or a circle or square. Once text is on the path, you can create special effects by flipping the text, creating a stair-step or rainbow effect with the characters, and more (**Figure 20a**).

**Figure 20a** Using the Type on a Path tool, we placed text on a circle, flipped it, and repositioned it. We then placed a picture on top of the circle.

## Placing Type on a Path

You can use any InDesign object, created with any tool, as a type path. Simply draw the shape and fill it or apply a stroke to it as you wish (see Chapter 5 and Chapter 7 for information about drawing and formatting objects). Once you have a path, click and hold the Type tool to display a pop-out menu, and then select the Type on a Path tool (**Figure 20b**).

**Figure 20b** Click and hold the Type tool to display a pop-out menu and select the Type on a Path tool.

With the Type on a Path tool selected, click the path where you want to start the text. While this sounds simple, it only works when the cursor is right over a path and a plus sign is displayed next to it (**Figure 20c**). Once you've successfully clicked on the path, start typing to add text. Change the font, size, color, alignment, and indents as usual (see #23 for more information).

<br />

**Figure 20c** To start typing on a path, select the Type on a Path tool and point at a path. When a plus sign (+) is displayed to the right of the cursor, click to start adding text to the path.

In addition to typing to add text to a path, you can import a text file (File > Place) or you can paste text from the clipboard. You can use either the Type on a Path tool or the Type tool to work with type on a path.

## Positioning Type on a Path

To create various effects, you can control where the text is placed relative to the path. Select the path with either the Selection tool or the Type on a Path tool and choose Type > Type on a Path > Options. The Type on a Path Options dialog box lets you choose a special effect for the characters, change how the text aligns with the path, adjust the spacing of characters, flip the text to the opposite side of the path, and more (**Figure 20d**).

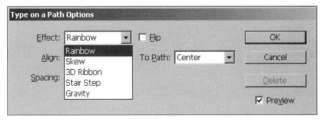

**Figure 20d** The Type on a Path Options dialog box lets you control how text is oriented to the path, including creating special effects with the characters such as Stair Step.

**Creating Boundaries for Type on a Path**

When you create type on a path, you can specify the boundaries for the text. To do this, click and drag the Type on a Path tool on the path rather than simply clicking it. As you drag, blue brackets display to indicate the start and endpoints of the type path.

If you want to adjust where text starts on the path, click the path with the Selection tool. Notice the blue bracket on each end of the text. These are similar to text frame edges in that they establish the left margin and the right margin for the text. You can drag these brackets with the Selection tool to reposition the start or endpoint of text on the path (**Figure 20e**). Also available is a center bracket, which you can drag across the path to flip text to the other side of the path or along the path to move all of the text.

### Tip
*You may need to zoom in to see and select the brackets.*

Figure 20e To change the starting position of text on a path, drag the start bracket to the left of the text. You can also drag the end bracket to compress the text area.

## Deleting Type on a Path
If you decide you no longer want type on a path, you can simply select the text and delete it. In this case, you can still add new text to the path. If you really don't want the path to be able to hold text, select it with the Selection tool or Direct Selection tool, and then choose Type > Type on a Path > Delete Type from Path.

# #21 Importing Text

Since most people compose documents in word processors, InDesign makes it easy to import Microsoft Word files and other text files. When importing text, you can customize how the text is imported (with or without formatting, for example), and you have various options for flowing it through a document. You can pretty much do anything from importing raw text with no formatting to bringing in fully formatted text that includes inline graphics, tables, a table of contents, an index, and footnotes.

## Placing a Text File

You can import text into an existing frame or type path—the frame doesn't even have to be a text frame because InDesign will automatically convert it. In addition, you can "load" the cursor with the imported text and create a new text frame. To import a text file:

1. If you want to import the text into an existing frame or type path, click in it. To flow text into the master text frame, press Command+Shift (Mac OS) or Ctrl+Shift (Windows) to select it. Otherwise, make sure no objects are selected.

2. Choose File > Place.

3. In the Place dialog box (**Figure 21**), locate and select the Microsoft Word or text file.

4. To customize how the text is imported, check Show Import Options. This gives you control over how much formatting and other elements are imported with the text.

5. If the selected frame contains text or a graphic and you want to replace it, check Replace Selected Item. If you uncheck this option, InDesign loads the cursor so you can create a new text frame.

6. Click Open.

### Supported Text File Formats

InDesign lets you import text files in .doc, .txt, and .rtf format. If you try to import a file from an unsupported version of Word, you will get an error message. Save the file as .rtf and reimport it—most of the formatting is still retained. InDesign also lets you import files from Microsoft Excel and in its own *Tagged Text* format. Tagged Text is exported from InDesign with proprietary tags that can be converted to actual formatting. Using Tagged Text is helpful for sharing formatted text among InDesign documents.

## Exporting Text Files

If you need to edit text outside InDesign, you can export it as Adobe InDesign Tagged Text, Rich Text Format, or Text Only. Using the Type tool, click in a story to export all of it or highlight the portions to export. Then, choose File > Export and select an option from the Format menu.

If the Missing Font alert displays, you can generally click OK to bypass the alert since you will be using formatting specified in InDesign. If, however, you plan to use the formatting in the file, note which fonts are missing and activate them using your font manager. You can also use the Find Font button to replace the fonts with active fonts.

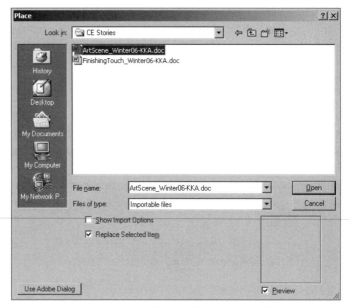

**Figure 21** The Place dialog box (File menu) lets you select Microsoft Word and text files to import.

## Setting Import Options

If you check Show Import Options in the Place dialog box, the Microsoft Word Import Options or Text Import Options dialog box displays. For Microsoft Word, you can use this dialog box to control whether the table of contents, inline graphics, formatting, and styles are imported along with the text and to resolve any style conflicts. For text files, you can clean up the text by removing extra paragraph returns and specify other options.

## Flowing Text Through a Document

When you import text into a selected frame, the text in the file fills the frame and automatically flows into all the frames threaded to it. If you selected the master text frame, pages and text frames are added as necessary to contain all the text.

If no frames are selected when you import text, the loaded text icon displays ⊞. At this point, you have three options:

- Click in a text frame or type path to flow the text into it.

- Click and drag to create a new text frame.

- Option+Shift-click (Mac OS) or Alt+Shift-click (Windows) to automatically create a text frame (within the margin guides) and flow the text into it. Any remaining text is overset. InDesign refers to this as *fixed-page autoflow*.

If all the text doesn't fit into the frame—as indicated by a red plus sign in the lower-right corner of the text frame—you have overset text. To flow the overset text through the document, you have several options:

- **Manual text flow:** Click an out port on the text frame to load the cursor again, and then create another text frame or thread this one to an existing text frame (see #19 for more information). With manual text flow, you need to continually reload the cursor and create new text frames or threads until all the text fits.

- **Semi-autoflow:** Option-click (Mac OS) or Alt-click (Windows) the loaded text icon to automatically reload the cursor. Thread text frames until all the text flows through the document.

- **Autoflow:** Shift-click the loaded text icon to add pages and text frames (based on the master text frame) until all the text fits.

Once you flow text, you may need to bump certain paragraphs or sections to a different column or page. Rather than using extra paragraph returns to do this, use the options in the Type > Insert Break Character submenu (such as Column Break or Page Break).

---

**Drag and Drop Importing**

In addition to using the Place command (File menu), InDesign lets you import both text and graphics files by dragging them from your computer desktop onto a page. If a frame is selected, the text or graphic is imported into the frame. If nothing is selected, a text frame is automatically created roughly where you drop the file.

# #22 Entering and Editing Text

Our first how-to for entering and editing text is mandatory—you need to use the Type tool or the Type on a Path tool. Our second how-to is voluntary but extremely helpful—choose Type > Show Hidden Characters. This displays invisible characters such as spaces, tabs, and paragraph returns so you can make precise selections, cut and paste more accurately, and prevent formatting errors (**Figure 22**). Other than these two how-tos, editing text in InDesign is pretty similar to using a word processor or even your email program.

**Figure 22** You can see a variety of hidden characters at work here: spaces are indicated by dots, tabs by double arrows, a dagger by an "indent here" character, paragraph returns by the traditional symbol ¶, and more.

## Positioning the Insertion Point

To start entering or editing text in a frame or a type path, you need an insertion point—aka, a flashing vertical cursor. To get this cursor, select the Type tool and click within any empty frame or within the text in a text frame. If the Selection tool or Direct Selection tool is selected, you can double-click a text frame to automatically select the Type tool and position the insertion point. To enter text in the master text frame, be sure to press Command+Shift (Mac OS) or Ctrl+Shift (Windows) while you click. Once you have an insertion point, you can begin typing or you can highlight text for editing and formatting.

### Tip
*If you cannot click in a text frame because it's behind other objects, use the Selection tool and press Command (Mac OS) or Ctrl (Windows) while you click. Keep clicking "through" other objects until the text frame is selected, and then switch to the Type tool. If this is an ongoing problem, place the text frame on its own layer (Window > Layers) for easy access.*

## Highlighting Text

To highlight text using the Type tool or the Type on a Path tool, click and drag the mouse. Other options include:

- Click twice to select a word.

- Click three times to select a line.

- Click four times to select a paragraph.

- Choose Edit > Select All to select the entire active story.

InDesign also provides a nifty way to highlight a range of text starting from the insertion point to another point in text. Click in the text and then Shift-click in another location—all the text is highlighted.

Once text is highlighted, you can cut, copy, and paste the night away.

## Editing Text

When text is highlighted, you can use standard Edit menu commands to Cut, Copy, and Paste the text to different locations. In addition, you can use the mouse to drag and drop text to different locations. Drag and drop is on by default for text in the Story Editor but off for text in layouts. To turn it on, open the Preferences dialog box, select the Type panel, and check Enable in Layout View in the Drag and Drop Text Editing Area.

To drag and drop text, first highlight it. Then, point at the text with the mouse to display the drag-and-drop icon ▸T. Drag the text to a new location indicated by the insertion point, and release the mouse button to drop it. When dragging and dropping text, you can create a new text frame or drop a copy of the text.

- To create a new frame for the text, press Command (Mac OS) or Ctrl (Windows) while you click and drag to create a new frame.

- To drop a copy of highlighted text, press Option (Mac OS) or Alt (Windows) when you release the mouse button to drop the text.

---

### Triple-clicking to Select Paragraphs

If you rarely select a single line but often select entire paragraphs, you can streamline the paragraph-selection process. In the Type panel in the Preference dialog box, uncheck Triple Click to Select a Line. When this is unchecked, clicking three times selects a paragraph (rather than four times).

# #23 Applying Character and Paragraph Formats

Here's where the fun starts—you get to start picking fonts, sizes, styles, and alignment to jazz up your text. InDesign's text formatting comes in two distinct flavors—character formats and paragraph formats. Character formats are attributes such as font and size that you can apply to individual characters. In fact, each character in a document can have its own unique formatting, although this sort of ransom-note style is not generally what graphic designers are aiming for. Paragraph formats are attributes such as indents and tabs that apply to entire paragraphs as opposed to individual characters. (If you can't tell where paragraphs begin and end, choose Type > Show Hidden Characters and look for the paragraph symbol ¶.)

Character formats and paragraph formats generally work together to complement the actual content. For example, weekly newsmagazines often use serif fonts and justified text to indicate authority, whereas an invitation to a fundraiser might be centered in a script font for an elegant look. While character formats account for the basic look of text—size, a serif or sans serif font—the formatting you apply to paragraphs largely controls the "color" of the type. This is not literally "color" as in whether it's black or blue, but the overall value of the type when you glance at a document or even look at it upside down. Are the blocks of text light and airy or dark and dense? Paragraph formats do this by controlling alignment, indents, space between paragraphs, hyphenation and justification, and more.

## Applying Character Formats

To apply character formats, highlight the text using the Type tool. Or, you can simply click in a text frame or on a type path and set character formats. The attributes will be applied when you start typing. All the character formats are available in the Character panel in the Control palette (**Figure 23a**). If you're not sure what an option does, point at it with the mouse to display its Tool Tip. Additional character formatting options are available in the palette menu.

**Figure 23a** The Character pane in the Control palette provides quick access to all the character formatting controls available in InDesign.

### Tearing Off the Character Palette

Having all the character formats in the Control palette may make the Character palette seem redundant. But if you find yourself switching back and forth between the Control palette's Character panel and Paragraph panel, you'll appreciate the availability of the Character palette. Simply drag its tab out of its palette to create an individual palette for it. You can then access both Paragraph and Character attributes at the same time. (You can also tear off the Paragraph palette and use the character options in the Control palette.)

If you prefer to work with the Character palette (Type menu), it offers a convenient place to specify basics: Font, Size, Leading, Kerning, and Tracking. Choose Show Options from the palette menu to expand the palette with more advanced options such as horizontal or vertical scaling and skewing (**Figure 23b**). The remaining character formatting options are available in the palette menu as well.

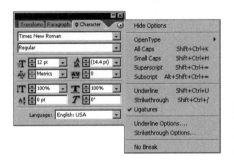

Figure 23b The Character palette also provides comprehensive character formats.

The only character formats you won't find here are color and stroke (see #34 for more information).

## Applying Paragraph Formats

To apply paragraph formats, use the Type tool and click in a paragraph to select it or highlight multiple paragraphs. All the paragraph formats are available in the Paragraph panel in the Control palette (**Figure 23c**). If you're not sure what an option does, point at it with the mouse to display its Tool Tip. Additional paragraph formatting options are available in the palette menu. Most of the paragraph formats are similar to those available in a word processor. InDesign, however, has a superior method of *composing* type, which is explained in #24.

Figure 23c The Paragraph pane in the Control palette provides quick access to all the paragraph formats available in InDesign.

In addition to using the Paragraph panel, you can use the Paragraph palette (Type menu). At its default size, it offers only alignment and indent controls, but you can choose Show Options from the palette menu to add more comprehensive paragraph formats.

**#23**: Applying Character and Paragraph Formats

## What Is Leading?

The space between lines in a paragraph—aka, leading—is usually a paragraph format. In InDesign, however, it's a character format. On the one hand, this is nice because most of the time you will modify size and leading in relation to each other. As a character format, the Font Size and Leading fields are right by each other. On the other hand, the reason leading is usually a paragraph format is that most of the time you want a consistent amount of space between lines in a paragraph. You don't want it to vary based on individual characters. InDesign offers the best of both worlds. While you always set leading as a character format, you can make it a paragraph format by checking Apply Leading to Entire Paragraphs in the Type panel in the Preferences dialog box.

# #24 Composing Type

**Experimenting with Composition**

To produce professional-looking type, the column width, Font, Size, and Leading settings will work together with the Hyphenation settings, Justification settings, and Adobe Paragraph Composer. You may need to experiment with this combination of character and paragraph formats to achieve the look you want.

Many of InDesign's character and paragraph formatting options are familiar to you from using a word processor—or even your email program. But what really sets InDesign apart is its superior method of text composition—of adjusting spacing and hyphenation to achieve evenly spaced type in a paragraph. The method is called the Adobe Paragraph Composer, and it works by considering spacing, hyphenation, and line breaks in all the lines in a paragraph in relation to each other. By contrast, the Adobe Single-line Composer and most other programs consider only one line at a time (**Figure 24a**).

Adobe Single-line Composer

I should've caught on the minute we got out of the car. From the parking lot, located just below Snowmass Ski Area, we were greeted by the sounds of hundreds of dogs—nearly 250, in fact—howling wildly from outside their kennels.

Adobe Paragraph Composer

I should've caught on the minute we got out of the car. From the parking lot, located just below Snowmass Ski Area, we were greeted by the sounds of hundreds of dogs—nearly 250, in fact—howling wildly from outside their kennels.

**Figure 24a** Although the difference between the Adobe Paragraph Composer and the Adobe Single-line Composer is subtle, the single-line method is more likely to produce inconsistent spacing. For example, at left, notice the spacing in the second line from the bottom—there are some gaps between words. At right, with the Adobe Paragraph Composer in use, you'll see more consistent spacing overall and particularly in the second-to-last line.

The three primary factors affecting composition—Hyphenation, Justification, and Composer—are paragraph formats and they are discussed here.

## Hyphenation

InDesign gives you far more control over automatic hyphenation than just turning it on and off for a paragraph. You can specify a limit to the number of lines in a row that end in hyphens, whether capitalized words can be hyphenated, the minimum number of letters a word must have to be hyphenated, the number of letters that must precede and follow a hyphen, and more. While these decisions impact the look of the text, they also have editorial implications, so you may want to set them with the help of an editor. For example, whether capitalized words should be hyphenated is often covered in the publisher's style guide and is not at the designer's discretion.

To set hyphenation, first select paragraphs with the Type tool. Then, choose Hyphenation from the Paragraph palette's menu (Type > Paragraph). You can also choose Hyphenation from the Control palette's menu when the Paragraph panel is displayed. The Hyphenation Settings dialog box (**Figure 24b**) lets you customize settings for the selected paragraphs. To see how changes affect the paragraphs, check the Preview box.

### Tip
*The Paragraph panel in the Control palette provides a Hyphenate check box so you can quickly turn hyphenation on and off.*

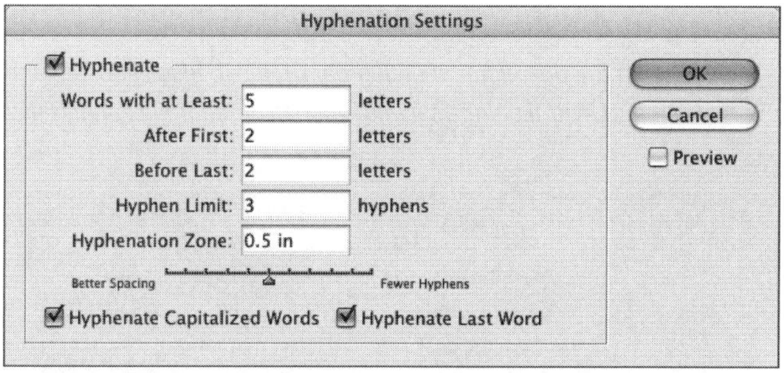

Figure 24b The Hyphenation Settings dialog box provides a slider for striking a balance between Better Spacing and Fewer Hyphens.

## Setting Justification

The Justification settings in InDesign control how spacing is adjusted in justified text, the leading, and which composition method is used. To set hyphenation, first select paragraphs with the Type tool. Then, choose Justification from the Paragraph palette's menu (Type > Paragraph). In the Justification dialog box (**Figure 24c**), be sure to check Preview to judge how your settings affect the text.

- **Word Spacing, Letter Spacing, and Glyph Scaling:** These fields control how spacing is adjusted and how characters are scaled when justifying text. (Therefore, these values do not apply to paragraphs that are right, left, or center aligned—only justified.)

*(continued on next page)*

---

### Use the Single-line Composer While Typing

Because the Adobe Paragraph Composer is continually considering spacing and line breaks throughout a paragraph, typing in a paragraph with it on can be slow and disconcerting. Text is continually reflowing, making it hard to concentrate on the words. To prevent this, edit the text in the Story Editor, which does not compose as you type (see #30).

- **Auto Leading:** This field controls the amount of space between lines in the selected paragraphs—if they use auto leading. The value is a percentage of the type size in use—so if the Font Size is 10 points, and Auto Leading is 120%, the Leading is set to 12 points.

- **Single Word Justification:** In justified text, if a single word falls on a line, you can specify how that word is handled by choosing an option from the Single Word Justification menu. Your options are to fully justify the word—possibly leading to giant gaps within the word—align it with the left margin, center it, or align it with the right margin.

- **Justification:** The dialog box also lets you select the Adobe Paragraph Composer or the Adobe Single-line Composer from the Composer menu.

*Tip*

*To open the Justification dialog box, you can also choose Justification from the Control palette's menu when the Paragraph panel is displayed.*

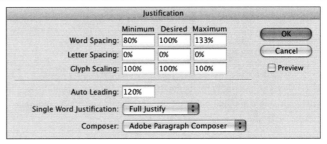

**Figure 24c** The Justification dialog box lets you fine-tune the spacing within justified paragraphs.

## Choosing a Composition Method

When paragraphs are selected with the Type tool, you can choose the Adobe Paragraph Composer or the Adobe Single-line Composer from the Paragraph palette's menu. You can also choose a composition method from the Composer menu in the Justification dialog box. The Adobe Paragraph Composer generally leads to better spacing, particularly in justified paragraphs.

# #25 Creating Bulleted and Numbered Lists

Lists are a great way to break up blocks of text, keeping text from both looking and sounding boring (**Figure 25a**). With features similar to those in Microsoft Word, InDesign makes it easy to create bulleted and numbered lists automatically. The feature, called Bullets and Numbering, is actually lifted from PageMaker. Aside from saving you the time of entering a bullet or number for each paragraph, formatting it, and specifying a tab and indent, the Bullets and Numbering feature creates lists that are easy to edit. For example, as you add paragraphs, bullets are added or numbers are inserted as necessary.

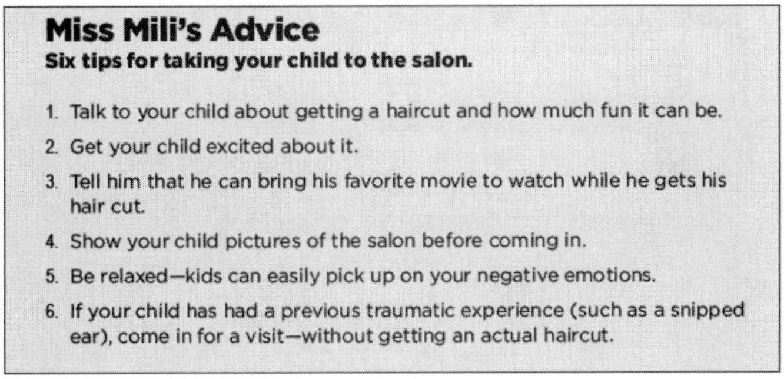

---

**Miss Mili's Advice**
Six tips for taking your child to the salon.

1. Talk to your child about getting a haircut and how much fun it can be.
2. Get your child excited about it.
3. Tell him that he can bring his favorite movie to watch while he gets his hair cut.
4. Show your child pictures of the salon before coming in.
5. Be relaxed—kids can easily pick up on your negative emotions.
6. If your child has had a previous traumatic experience (such as a snipped ear), come in for a visit—without getting an actual haircut.

---

**Figure 25a** Clicking the Numbered List button in the PageMaker toolbox created this list.

To create a bulleted or numbered list:

**1.** Highlight the paragraphs with the Type tool.

**2.** Display the Paragraph panel in the Control palette (or choose Type > Paragraph to display the Paragraph palette).

**3.** Choose Bullets and Numbering from the palette menu.

**4.** In the Bullets and Numbering dialog box (**Figure 25b**), choose an option from the List Type menu at the top: Bullets or Numbers.

*(continued on next page)*

## Bulleted and Numbered List Buttons

If the PageMaker toolbox (Window menu) is showing, you can click the Bulleted List or Numbered List button to quickly add bullets or numbers to highlighted paragraphs. The formatting is based on the current settings in the Bullets and Numbering dialog box.

5. Choose a type of bullet or number. When working with bullets, click the Add button to access a character map and select new bullet characters. When working with numbers, you can specify a Style (1, 2, 3 or i, ii, iii, for example), Separator (such as a period), and a Start At number.

6. Use the menus to choose a Font Family, Font Style, Size, and Color.

7. In the Bullet or Number Position area, choose Hanging or Flush Left from the Position menu and specify the indents.

After you've created a bulleted or numbered list, you can change any of the settings by highlighting the paragraphs and opening the Bullets and Numbering dialog box again.

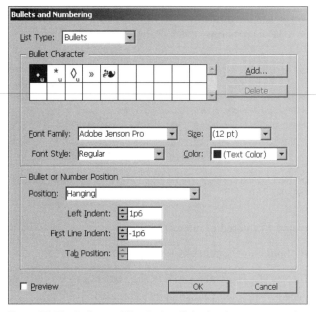

**Figure 25b** The Bullets and Numbering dialog box lets you customize the formatting of automatic bulleted and numbered lists.

# #26 Setting Tabs

You're no doubt familiar with tabs from your typewriter days—if you had them—but they're even more important in a page layout environment. To align text horizontally, it's important to use tabs rather than spaces for precision alignment. Unlike characters on a typewriter, the width of characters and spaces in fonts can vary, making it impossible to align text.

InDesign provides default tab settings at every half inch, but you're not stuck with those. You can override the default tabs and customize each tab stop by specifying how text aligns with it and adding *leader* characters (**Figure 26a**).

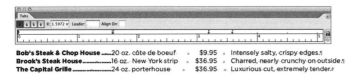

| Bob's Steak & Chop House | 20 oz. côte de boeuf | » | $9.95 | » | Intensely salty, crispy edges.¶ |
| Brook's Steak House | 16 oz. New York strip | » | $36.95 | » | Charred, nearly crunchy on outside.¶ |
| The Capital Grille | 24 oz. porterhouse | » | $36.95 | » | Luxurious cut, extremely tender.# |

**Figure 26a** This text is divided into three columns with three different tab stops. The first tab stop is left aligned with a dot leader; the second tab stop aligns to the decimal point in the prices; the third tab stop is left-aligned again.

Tabs are paragraph formats, so they apply to selected paragraphs rather than individual lines within a paragraph or characters. To set tabs:

1. Choose Type > Show Hidden Characters to view tab characters in text. They look like double arrows.

2. Select the Type tool.

3. Highlight the paragraphs you want to set tabs for.

4. Choose Type > Tabs to open the Tabs palette.

5. Click one of the alignment buttons at the top left to specify how text aligns with the tab stop: left-justified, center-justified, right-justified, or align to decimal. If you click align to decimal, you can actually specify any alignment character, such as a comma, in the Align On field at right.

*(continued on next page)*

## Repeating a Tab Stop

If you want to create a series of tab stops that are a specific distance apart, you can use the Repeat command in the Tabs palette menu. For example, if you have a tab stop at .75 inches and you'd like another one at 1.5 inches, select the tab stop and .75 and choose Repeat. The alignment and any leader characters are copied as well.

6. If you want to fill the white space created by the tab with a character, you can enter up to eight characters to repeat in the Leader field. For example, if you want periods to lead the eye from a table of contents entry to its page number, enter a period in the field. For more space between the periods, enter a period and a space.

7. Click the ruler where you want to place the tab. The X field displays the position. Once you set a tab stop, all the default tab stops to the left of it are cleared.

To modify a tab stop, click its icon on the tab ruler and change any of its settings (for example, click a different alignment button). To delete a tab stop, drag its icon off the ruler. To delete all tab stops, choose Clear All from the Tabs palette's menu.

InDesign provides a "Right Indent Tab," which forces text over to the paragraph's right-indent value. The Right Indent Tab is particularly useful for positioning an "end of story" character or an author's initials (**Figure 26b**). To insert it, choose Type > Insert Special Character > Right Indent Tab.

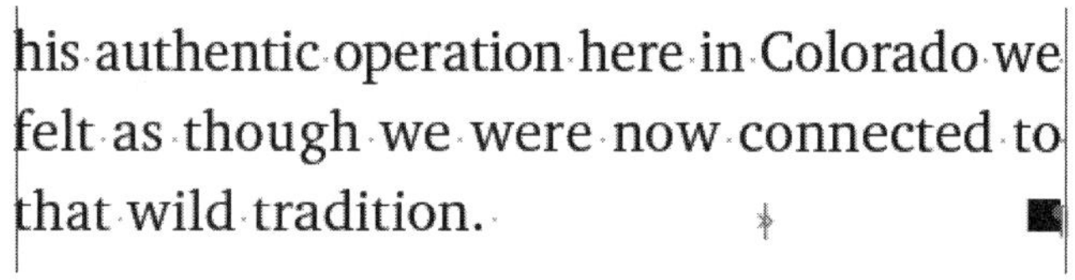

his authentic operation here in Colorado we felt as though we were now connected to that wild tradition.

Figure 26b To automatically align an "end-of-story" character with the right-indent of the paragraph, insert a Right Indent Tab rather than a standard tab.

# #27 Setting Text Defaults

Whenever you start typing in a new text frame or on a new type path, InDesign applies the formatting specified in the default paragraph style, which is called Basic Paragraph. You can override the settings in the Basic Paragraph style by making changes in the Paragraph and Character panels in the Control palette before you start typing. You can modify this default formatting for the active document or for all new documents.

## Editing the Basic Paragraph Style

To modify the Basic Paragraph style:

1. Choose Type > Paragraph Styles.

2. In the Paragraph Styles palette, double-click Basic Paragraph.

3. Change any options in the panels in the Paragraph Style Options dialog box (**Figure 27a**).

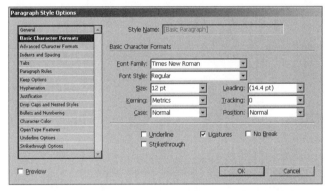

Figure 27a The Basic Character Formats panel in the Paragraph Style Options dialog box lets you specify the font, size, leading, and other character formats for the default Basic Paragraph style.

## Overriding the Basic Paragraph Style

Before you start typing, you can override the settings in the Basic Paragraph Style. With the Type tool selected, you can make changes in the Character panel and the Paragraph panel in the Control palette. In addition, you can make changes in the Character palette (**Figure 27b**) and the Paragraph palette, both of which are available in the Type menu.

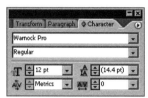

**Figure 27b** Override the Basic Paragraph Style character formats by making changes in either the Character panel in the Control palette or the Character palette (Type menu).

# #28 Working with Fonts

As you no doubt know from working on a computer, fonts define the look of characters. If you're an experienced graphic designer, you may not need to know much about fonts other than how they're handled in InDesign. If you're new to graphic design, however, we'll cover the basics of fonts for you.

## Applying a Font

Fonts are character formats that you apply as follows:

1. Select the Type tool.

2. Highlight the text you want to apply a font to.

3. On the left side of the Control palette's Character pane (**Figure 28**), choose an option from the Font menu or enter a font name in the field. The menu displays a preview of the font next to the name so you can see what it looks like.

4. Below the Font menu, you can choose an option from the Style menu—for example, Bold, Semibold, Italic, or Oblique. These are the styles activated on your system for the font—they do not come from InDesign.

You can also choose fonts from the same menus in the Character palette (Type menu).

**Figure 28** The far left side of the Control palette's Character pane provides the Font and Style menus.

## Checking Fonts

When you open documents, InDesign checks to see that all the fonts are active on your system. If they're not, you're notified so you can activate or replace them. If you need to change the fonts used in a document, you can use Type > Find Font to search and replace them. When you're ready for output, use File > Package to have InDesign collect copies of fonts to provide to the printer.

### Using an Auto-Activation Plug-in

Font managers such as Suitcase, Suitcase Fusion, and FontAgent Pro offer free plug-ins that automatically activate fonts as you open documents. This can be a significant benefit of purchasing a font manager rather than using the utility provided with your system to activate fonts. If you're looking to buy a font manager, check to see if it provides an auto-activation plug-in for InDesign CS2. These plug-ins are more available for Mac OS users than for Windows users.

**Applying OpenType Styles**

If you're using an OpenType font, additional style options may be built into it from the font designer. These styles may include fancy typographic effects such as Fractions, Discretionary Ligatures, Slashed Zero, and Proportional Old Style numerals. To see if any options are available for the active font, choose OpenType from the Character palette's menu. Any options in brackets in the Open-Type submenu are not available for the font. You can choose the other options as applicable—for example, if Fractions is available, you might apply it to "1/2" but not to words. You can identify OpenType fonts by the black-and-green "O" preceding the font name; the name often ends with "Pro" as well.

# Font Basics

If you've ever uttered the sentence, "My computer doesn't have that font" (and you're not sure what's wrong with saying that), this section is for you. Since many fonts do come with your computer and even more come with programs you buy, it's easy to think that fonts are part of the computer or a specific program. But it's not true. Fonts are independent files that you can turn on (activate) and off (deactivate) through your system or a font management program. You can buy additional fonts from manufacturers such as Adobe, Linotype, and Bitstream and add them to your system.

Fonts come in a variety of formats, including PostScript, Open-Type, and TrueType. Currently, the most widely used and accepted fonts are PostScript Type 1—in fact, you may encounter complaints from other users and printers if you don't use them. OpenType fonts, however, are gaining ground because they can contain thousands of characters and are cross-platform (meaning the same file can be used on Mac OS and Windows systems).

Whichever fonts you use in whatever format, the most important thing to remember is consistency. It's likely that your computer has multiple versions of the same font—Times, Helvetica, Palatino—in various formats from different vendors. To prevent text from reflowing, the exact fonts you use to design a document should be used each time you edit it. And those same fonts should be sent along to the printer.

# #29 Using Paragraph and Character Styles

When formatting an entire document, you're certainly not expected to remember and consistently apply the hundreds of paragraph and character formats InDesign provides. Instead, you can create paragraph styles and character styles to apply multiple formats to text with a single click or keyboard shortcut. And, if you change a format in a style, it's changed everywhere the style is used. For example, you can change a font in a style and it will automatically change throughout a document. Using styles has so many benefits in terms of speed and consistency that you'd never want to work on a long document such as a book, magazine, or newsletter without them.

## Creating Styles

Paragraph styles apply to entire paragraphs and include both paragraph formats and character formats. Character styles, on the other hand, specify only character formats and are applied to highlighted text. Character styles are useful for special formatting within a paragraph. For example, corporate stock symbols in body copy are often formatted to stand out through the use of small caps, a sans serif font, and maybe a different color. You create paragraph and character styles in the same way, but from different palettes.

Generally, the best way to create styles is to first format sample text that includes all the different styles you will need for a document, such as heads, subheads, indented paragraphs, paragraphs with no indent, bulleted lists, and so on. Then, use the formatted text as a basis for the styles.

To create a style:

1. Using the Type tool, highlight formatted text.

2. Choose Type > Paragraph Styles or Type > Character Styles.

3. From the palette menu, choose New Paragraph Style or New Character Style.

*(continued on next page)*

## Preceding Style Names with Numbers

The Character Styles and Paragraph Styles palettes list styles in alphabetical order. However, many designers prefer to list styles according to usage, with heads first, subheads and body text styles second, and lesser-used styles such as photo credits toward the bottom. To achieve this organization, precede style sheet names with numbers such as "1 Head," "1a Subhead," and "2 Body." You can then synchronize the keyboard shortcuts to the numbers by using Control+1 for Heads and Control+Shift+1 for Subheads, for example. If a document has a many styles to scroll through, you can further streamline the list by choosing Small Palette Rows from the palette menu.

**4.** In the Paragraph Style Options dialog box (**Figure 29a**) or the Character Style Options dialog box, enter a name for the style.

**5.** To apply the style using a keyboard shortcut, click in the Shortcut field and press the shortcut keys you want to assign. Generally, it's best to use the modifier keys and the numbers on the keypad as shortcuts.

**6.** All the formatting options are already set according to the formatted text as summarized in the Style Settings area. Click in the scroll list at left to display panels of options and change any of the formatting.

If you're not working with formatted text, you can create a new style by clicking the New button at the bottom of the Paragraph Styles or Character Styles palette. This creates a new style in the palette called Paragraph Style 1 or Character Style 1. The number reflects the creation order. Double-click the new style to name and modify it.

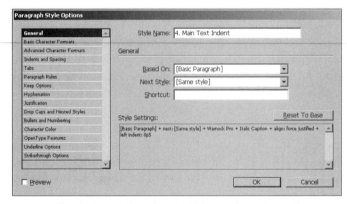

**Figure 29a** The Paragraph Style Options dialog box lets you specify a name, shortcut key, and formatting for a new paragraph style.

## Applying Styles

Applying styles is easy: Select the text and click the style name or press its keyboard shortcut.

- To apply a paragraph style, click in a paragraph or highlight several paragraphs with the Type tool. Click the style name in the Paragraph Styles palette (**Figure 29b**) or press the keyboard shortcut shown for it.

- To apply a character style, highlight text with the Type tool. Click the style name in the Character Styles palette (**Figure 29c**) or press its keyboard shortcut.

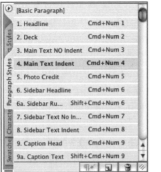
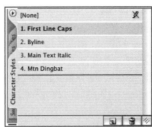

**Figures 29b and 29c** Click style names in the Paragraph Styles palette (left) and the Character Styles palette (right) to apply them to selected text.

Occasionally, a paragraph's formatting may start to "wander" from the formatting specified in its paragraph style. For example, you might track in text to make it fit in a frame, only to have the text cut later. Any formatting that does not match the style is called an "override." To force a paragraph's formatting to match its original paragraph style, select it and choose Clear Overrides from the palette menu. You can also Option-click (Mac OS) or Alt-click a style name. Note that this does not remove character styles applied within the paragraph.

## Modifying Styles

To change the formatting specified in a style, you can double-click the style name or select the style name and choose Style Options from the Character or Paragraph palette menus. Or, as a shortcut, reformat some of the text in the style, and then choose Redefine Style from the palette menu. The Character and Paragraph palette menus also provide options for duplicating, deleting, importing, and exporting styles.

# #30 Using the Story Editor

Part of the beauty of working in InDesign is the way you can truly see your pages coming together—the way the type and graphics work together to communicate a message. However, sometimes you need to revise the text of the message, and all those graphics can simply get in the way. To get around this, InDesign provides the Story Editor, which lets you edit plain text in a separate window. If you've ever worked in PageMaker or reviewed "galleys," the Story Editor will be familiar to you.

Using the Story Editor is particularly helpful when you're working with reverse type, complex text wraps, or text placed behind other semitransparent objects. Anytime you're having trouble working with text, select a text frame in the story and choose Edit > Edit in Story Editor (**Figure 30**). All the text in the story is displayed in a separate window that includes a list of paragraph styles applied to text, a vertical depth ruler, and an overset text indicator.

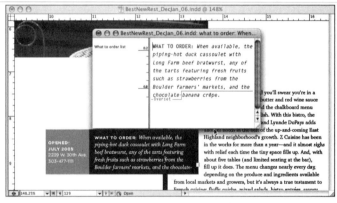

**Figure 30** The Story Editor (Edit > Edit in Story Editor) makes it easy to focus on editing text while seeing the impact of your edits on the layout.

When you're in a Story Editor window, the Type tool is automatically selected so you can edit the text as usual. You will see only the most basic formatting attributes, such as bold and italics; tables, inline objects, footnotes, and the like are represented by icons. While you're editing text in the Story Editor, you can see changes in the layout as well.

You can open multiple stories in their own Story Editor windows, including opening a Story Editor for a type path. The Story Editor windows work as follows:

- Drag the Story Editor window and document window as necessary for the most convenient positioning. For example, you might place them side by side to see how text changes affect a column in the layout.

- Each open Story Editor window is listed at the bottom of the Window menu. If the window you're working on goes behind the document window, choose it from the Window menu to bring it forward.

- If you're working with a text frame containing overset text, a line indicates where the text no longer fits in the frame.

- Use the View > Story Editor submenu to control what displays in the Story Editor: Style Name Column, Depth Ruler, and Footnotes. These commands affect all open Story Editor windows.

- If the Style Name Column is displayed, you can drag the divider to adjust the column width.

When you're finished working in a Story Editor window, close it or choose Edit > Edit in Layout.

**Customizing the Story Editor**

If you don't like the Story Editor's font or background color, you can change it in the Story Editor Display panel in the Preferences dialog box. You can further customize the Story Editor by changing the font size, line spacing, text color, anti-aliasing setting, and cursor type.

# #31 Checking Spelling

InDesign's spelling checker is incredibly sophisticated. You can check anything from a text selection to multiple documents, check against spelling dictionaries in most major languages, customize the spelling dictionaries, and more. In addition to flagging words that do not appear in its dictionaries, InDesign also flags duplicated words and possible capitalization errors. We have to warn you, though, that the spelling checker is not foolproof. It doesn't know what words you intended to use—there, their, or they're—and it doesn't understand context. When making decisions about possible misspelled words, it's best if you work with a copy editor or proofreader.

## Running a Spelling Checker

You can check spelling in selected text, to the end of a story, in an entire story or document, and in all open documents. If you want to check a limited amount of text, you need to first prepare the document by highlighting a range of text with the Type tool, clicking within a story to check it from that point forward, or selecting a text frame to check the entire story.

To check spelling, choose Edit > Spelling > Check Spelling. Choose an option from the Search menu to specify the scope of the spelling checker: All Documents, Document, Story, To End of Story, or Selection. When a word displays in the field at the top of the dialog box (**Figure 31a**), handle it as follows:

- **If you think the word is spelled incorrectly:** Select a word in the Suggested Corrections list or enter the correct spelling in the Change To field. Then, click Change to fix the first instance of the word or click Change All to fix all instances of the word without reviewing them first.

- **If the word is spelled correctly:** Click Skip to continue to check spelling. If you know the word is used multiple times in the document and you don't want to click Skip each time, click Ignore All.

The Check Spelling dialog box is actually a palette, so you can jump into the document and edit the text without closing it. When you're finished checking spelling, click Done.

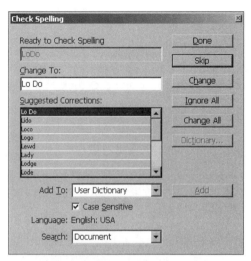

Figure 31a The Check Spelling dialog box helps you find the correct spelling for words.

### Checking Spelling in Different Languages

InDesign is not limited to checking spelling in English. To tell InDesign which language dictionary to use for a range of text, highlight the text and then choose an option from the Language menu in the Control palette's Character pane. For example, if you highlight "crème brûlée" and then choose French from the Language menu, InDesign will consult its French dictionary and determine that it is spelled correctly.

## Customizing the Dictionary

If we know anything about a spelling checker, we know that it's not infallible. For one thing, the dictionary rarely recognizes all the unique words in your content, including the names of people, places, brands, foods, and more. If you frequently work with the same content—and are constantly skipping or ignoring the same words—you can add those words to the document's dictionary or to your user dictionary. Customizing the dictionary not only results in fewer flagged words, but it also helps ensure that you don't spell proper names wrong.

You have two options for customizing the dictionary:

- While you're in the Check Spelling dialog box, click Add. The word in the field is added to the dictionary listed in the Add To field. By default, this is your user dictionary, but you can choose to add the word to a dictionary that is unique to the active document. If the word requires specific capitalization—such as "LoDo," the abbreviation for Denver's Lower Downtown neighborhood—make sure Case Sensitive is checked when you click Add.

*(continued on next page)*

- Choose Edit > Spelling > Dictionary (or click Dictionary in the Check Spelling dialog box). In the Dictionary dialog box (**Figure 31b**), choose whether to edit the user dictionary or the document dictionary from the Target menu. Enter correctly spelled words in the Word field, check or uncheck Case Sensitive, and then click Add.

To edit words in the dictionary, select the word and click Remove. Then retype the word in the Word field and click Add.

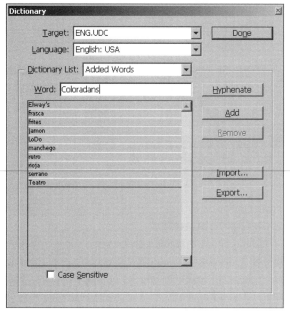

**Figure 31b** The Dictionary dialog box lets you customize the user dictionary or the document's dictionary.

## Setting Spelling Preferences

By default, the InDesign Check Spelling command flags words that it thinks are misspelled, words it thinks should be capitalized, and duplicate words. If this results in too many flagged words, you can customize Check Spelling in the Spelling panel in the Preferences dialog box. The check boxes work as follows:

- **Misspelled Words** flags words that do not match words in the current language dictionary.

- **Repeated Words** flags duplicate words such as "in in."

- **Uncapitalized Words** flags words that are capitalized in the dictionary but not in the document.

- **Uncapitalized Sentences** flags lowercase words following a period, exclamation point, or question mark.

You might, for example, uncheck Uncapitalized Words and Uncapitalized Sentences if a design-intensive document uses all lowercase for effect.

# #32 Correcting Spelling Automatically

If you've ever used Microsoft Word's AutoCorrect features, you've probably noticed that as you're typing it will fix blatant mistakes you make and underline words it doesn't recognize. For example, if you type "teh," it changes it to "the." If you type "InDesign," it underlines it to let you know that it might be misspelled. InDesign works the same way—except the automatic spelling correction and the underlining of possibly misspelled words are both turned off by default. You can easily turn these features on and off as you need them, and they are both customizable.

## Using Autocorrect

To automatically correct common misspellings as you type, choose Edit > Spelling > Autocorrect. You can also check Enable Autocorrect in the Autocorrect panel in the Preferences dialog box. The Autocorrect panel lets you edit InDesign's default list of common misspellings as well. Note that Autocorrect is not retroactive—it will not go through existing text and correct it. It works only as you type.

## Underlining Unrecognized Words

To have InDesign underline spelling issues, choose Edit > Spelling > Dynamic Spelling. By default, squiggly red lines underline possible misspellings and squiggly green lines underline duplicated words and potential capitalization errors. For possible misspellings, you can Control-click (Mac OS) or right-click (Windows) to display a context menu (**Figure 32**). You can choose from a list of suggested spellings, add the spelling to the user dictionary, or ignore all instances of the spelling. If you choose Add or Ignore All from the context menu, the word is no longer underlined.

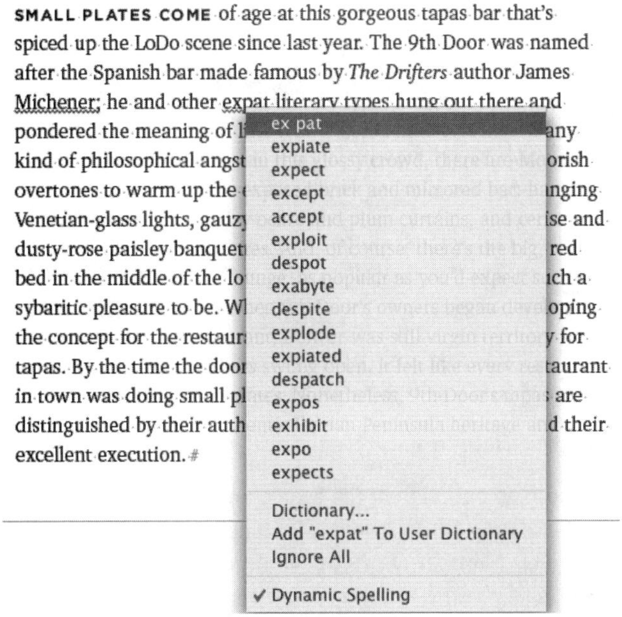

**SMALL PLATES COME** of age at this gorgeous tapas bar that's spiced up the LoDo scene since last year. The 9th Door was named after the Spanish bar made famous by *The Drifters* author James Michener; he and other expat literary types hung out there and pondered the meaning of l̲i̲f̲e̲. any kind of philosophical angst orish overtones to warm up the nging Venetian-glass lights, gauzy ise and dusty-rose paisley banquet red bed in the middle of the lo ich a sybaritic pleasure to be. W oping the concept for the restaur for tapas. By the time the door taurant in town was doing small pl are distinguished by their auth d their excellent execution. #

| |
|---|
| **ex pat** |
| expiate |
| expect |
| except |
| accept |
| exploit |
| despot |
| exabyte |
| despite |
| explode |
| expiated |
| despatch |
| expos |
| exhibit |
| expo |
| expects |
| Dictionary... |
| Add "expat" To User Dictionary |
| Ignore All |
| ✓ Dynamic Spelling |

**Figure 32** InDesign does not recognize "Michener" nor "expat" so it underlines both. Displaying a context menu lets you choose a different spelling, add it to your dictionary, or ignore it.

## Using Autocorrect as a Macro

While Autocorrect is handy for fixing mistakes, you can also use it as a poor man's macro to save yourself keystrokes. If you type the same phrase over and over—"at 5,280 feet in the mile-high city" for example—you could have InDesign Autocorrect instances of "a5ft" to actually read "at 5,280 feet in the mile-high city."

# #33 Searching and Replacing Text

## Using a Wild Card

If you want to find multiple variations of a word, you can enter a wild card character. For example, to find "run" and "ran," enter the wild card for the vowel. The wild card symbol is a carat (Shift+6) followed by a question mark: ^?.

Nothing is more tedious than having to make global changes in text. Say that an editor suddenly decides that all instances of "5280" need to be "5,280." Then say the designer decides that all instances of "5280" need to be in Cheltenham Red. The quickest, most foolproof way to handle these changes is through InDesign's Find/Change feature. To use Find/Change:

1. Choose Edit > Find/Change. This opens the Find/Change palette, so you can jump into the text and edit it without closing the palette.

2. In the Find What area, type the text you want to find. (You can leave this blank if you simply want to change formatting.)

3. In the Change To area, type the text you want to replace it with.

4. Choose an option from the Search menu to specify the scope of your search: All Documents, Document, Story, To End of Story, and Selection. (If necessary, you can jump into the document and select a story, an insertion point, or text to search.)

5. Check Whole Word if you don't want to find variations of the Find What text (such as plurals).

6. Check Case Sensitive if you only want to find text with the exact capitalization pattern shown in the Find What field. When this option is checked, the capitalization in the Change To field is used for changes as well.

7. If you want to consider formatting in the search, click the More Options button to expand the Find/Change palette (**Figure 33**).

8. Use the Format buttons in the Find Format Settings and Change Format Settings area to specify the formatting you want to find and replace.

9. Click Find Next to start the search. When you locate the found text, click Change to replace it with the Change To text and formatting or click Find Next again to skip it.

**10.** Click Find Next to continue the search. After you click Change and confirm that the changes are correct, you can click Change All to change all instances within the search scope.

When you're finished with the Find/Change palette, click Done.

**Filling Find What and Change To**

Since Find/Change relies on your accuracy in entering information in the Find What and Change To fields, you can paste text into both fields. (If drag and drop is enabled for the layout, you can also drop text in the fields.) If the text is formatted, its formatting is automatically selected in the Find Format Settings and Change Format Settings areas. Pasting is particularly helpful when you want to Find/Change special characters such as tabs. The Find What and Change To fields also include menus that list your most recent operations.

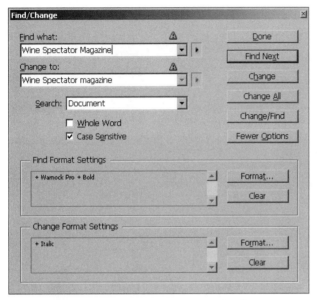

**Figure 33** This search will find all instances of "Wine Spectator Magazine" in the document and replace it with "Wine Spectator magazine" in italics.

# CHAPTER FOUR

# Typography and Tables

It's hard to say when you go from "working with text" to focusing on "typography," where your primary concern is the style, arrangement, and appearance of the text. Some of the basic decisions you make, such as font and size, affect typography, but the real reason you use InDesign is for all the options it provides for fine-tuning. This includes text within tables, which are often ideal for presenting information. Judicious use of features discussed in this chapter can give your projects a professional edge.

In this chapter, you'll learn how to apply special effects such as scaling type, creating drop caps, anchoring objects in text, wrapping text around objects and images, and more. In addition, you'll look at features for creating and formatting tables that save you time and enhance your design.

# #34 Special Effects for Type

The look of type is largely dependent on the typeface you select (serif, sans serif, script, etc.), the style (bold, italic, bold italic, etc.), and the size. The spacing between characters, words, lines, and paragraphs will impact the design as well. But for serious impact, you might experiment with some of InDesign's special effects, such as stroke, color, scale, and skew. These options generally work best with smaller blocks of text such as headlines or pull quotes: You wouldn't, for example, apply a stroke to an entire page of body text unless you wanted to give your readers a headache. (Note that two special effects are discussed in other chapters; see #20 for type on a path and #65 for drop shadows.)

## Applying a Style

When type is highlighted, you can apply a style to characters by clicking buttons in the Character panel in the Control palette. Next to the Font Size and Leading fields, you'll find buttons for All Caps, Small Caps, Superscript, Subscript, Underline, and Strikethrough. These commands are also available in the Character palette menu.

## Applying a Stroke and Color

When text is highlighted with the Type tool, you can *stroke* or outline its edges, and you can change its color. To stroke text, enter a value in the Weight field in the Stroke palette (Window menu). To change the color of text, click a color swatch in the Swatches palette (Window menu). When working with the Swatches palette, if necessary click the Formatting Affects Text button (**Figure 34a**); use the Stroke/Fill button in the upper-left corner to control whether the color applies to the stroke or the body of the characters.

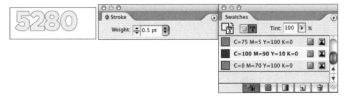

Figure 34a The Stroke palette lets you outline highlighted characters, and the Swatches palette lets you apply a color to them.

## Scaling Text

To achieve certain design effects, you might want to horizontally scale (expand) or vertically scale (condense) text. Since scale distorts the text, it is usually reserved for increasing the visual impact of display type such as headline. Some designers, however, will scale text a tiny bit (such as 97% vertically) for copyfitting purposes. You have two options for scaling text, numerically or visually:

- Using the Type tool, highlight the text, and then enter a percent value in the Horizontal Scale or Vertical Scale field in the Character palette (**Figure 34b**) or the Character pane in the Control palette.

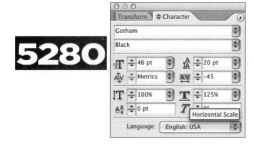

**Figure 34b**
The Vertical Scale and Horizontal Scale fields let you condense and expand text, respectively.

- Using the Scale tool, drag a corner of the text frame to resize it (**Figure 34c**). All the text scales automatically, scaling vertically if you decrease the frame width and scaling horizontally if you increase the frame width. As a shortcut to selecting the Scale tool, you can press Command (Mac OS) or Ctrl (Windows) while using the Selection tool.

**Figure 34c** Dragging the corner of a text frame with the Scale tool will scale the text as you resize the frame.

### Use the Appropriate Font Face

When you select a typeface in InDesign, such as Helvetica, an adjacent menu lets you select a style such as Condensed, Expanded, or Italic. In general, it is better to use the font style rather than scaling or skewing type because you benefit from alterations the font designer made to the spacing and characters. Scaling and skewing work best for creating special effects.

## Skewing Type

InDesign can *skew* or slant type to somewhat mimic italics. To do this, highlight text with the Type tool and enter a value in the Skew field in the Character palette (**Figure 34d**) or the Character pane in the Control palette. Skew is expressed in degrees with positive values skewing text to the right and negative values skewing text to the left.

**Figure 34d** The Skew field lets you enter a value in degrees to slant type to the right or left.

## Converting Type to Outlines

If you just cannot achieve the look you want by adjusting the font, stroke, color, scale, or skew of type, you can convert the characters to a frame shaped like the characters. You can then fill the frame with text or a graphic. To do this, highlight the text with the Type tool (you can only convert one line of text at a time) and choose Type > Create Outlines. The new frame is automatically anchored in the surrounding text. To remove an anchored object, select the frame with the Selection tool, choose Edit > Cut, and deselect the text frame. Then, choose Edit > Paste.

# #35 Setting Up Drop Caps and Nested Styles

Look at the first paragraph of a story in just about any magazine. Usually, at least the first letter is enlarged and embellished in some way to pull your eyes into the paragraph. In graphic design, this is referred to as a *drop cap*. In addition to the drop cap, the first few words or the first line might look different, with all caps or small caps a common choice, although a font switch is becoming more common. InDesign refers to this as a *nested style*.

Although they appear to be applied to specific characters, both drop caps and nested styles are paragraph formats. The benefit of this is that you can use a paragraph style to apply both formats with a single click—and the formats are not dependent on any specific text. You can edit text and even delete the first character of a paragraph, and the drop cap remains, for example. The nested style formatting might be set up to change the font of the first four words or to the end of the first sentence. Again, changing the text will not remove the nested style formatting.

## Creating Drop Caps

To create a drop cap:

1. Click in a paragraph with the Type tool to select it.

2. In the Paragraph palette (Type menu) or the Paragraph panel in the Control palette (**Figure 35a**), locate the Drop Cap Number of Lines ⁣⬛ and Drop Cap One or More Characters ⬛ fields.

3. In the Drop Cap Number of Lines field, enter the number of lines you want the drop caps to drop into. For example, if you enter 3, the drop caps become large enough to drop down into the first three lines of the paragraph.

*(continued on next page)*

## Using Paragraph Styles

For quick and consistent application of drop caps and nested styles, save the settings in a paragraph style. Be sure to create any character styles you will need first (for additional drop cap formatting or for the nested style formatting). In the Paragraph Style Options dialog box, use the Drop Caps and Nested Style panel to set up how the first few characters and/or lines of the paragraph should look. See #29 for more information about paragraph styles.

**4.** In the Drop Cap One or More Characters field, enter how many characters you want to become drop caps. Generally, you will only see one-character drop caps, but sometimes the number is adjusted based on the context. For example, it might be modified so the entire first word of a paragraph becomes the drop cap (and therefore you have to set the value for each paragraph). Or, if you usually use one drop cap but the first character in a paragraph is an open quotation mark, you might adjust that paragraph to have a two-character drop cap.

Once you have created drop caps for a paragraph, you can still highlight those characters and apply character attributes or a character style. It's pretty common to see a font or color change in a drop cap.

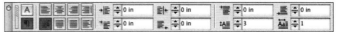

**W**HEN I DECIDED to embark on my first dog-sledding trip, with Krabloonik Kennels in Snowmass Village, one of the few places in the continental United States to experience the sport, I anticipated an experience straight out of a Christmas TV special. My husband and I would be snuggled together, covered with blankets in a sleigh

**Figure 35a** The Paragraph panel in the Control palette provides control over how many characters are treated as drop caps and how deep they drop into the paragraph.

## Creating Nested Styles

In addition to creating drop caps manually, you can create them through the Drop Caps and Nested Styles dialog box (**Figure 35b**). This not only lets you specify how many characters should drop and how many lines, but you can automatically apply a character style as well. In addition, you can apply a character style to the beginning of the paragraph, for example, to change the first line or first sentence to all caps.

To set up this formatting, create any character styles you will need for the drop cap and for the nested style. Then click in the paragraph and choose Drop Caps and Nested Styles from the menu in the Paragraph panel in the Control palette or the Paragraph palette.

- **Drop Caps area:** Set up the drop cap in the Lines and Characters fields. To apply additional formatting to the drop caps through a character style, choose it from the Character Style menu.

- **Nested Styles area:** To specify formatting for the beginning of the paragraph, click New Nested Style at the bottom of the dialog box. Select the character style for the text first, and then use the next three fields to specify how much text to apply it to. For example, you might apply a bold font to the first three words in a paragraph. Or, you might apply a different color up to an em space. You can create more than one nested style for a paragraph, which is helpful for formatting single-line paragraphs in a table of contents, for example.

Note that you do not have to use both drop caps and nested styles: The dialog box lets you set up one or the other or both.

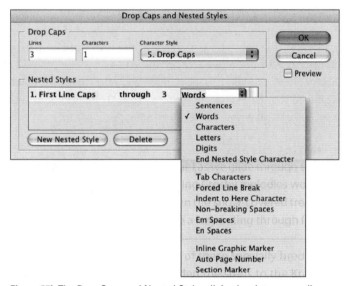

**Figure 35b** The Drop Caps and Nested Styles dialog box lets you easily apply formatting to the beginning of paragraphs, including drop caps and style switches such as small caps or bold.

# #36 Inserting Special Characters and Glyphs

Many of the special typographic features within fonts—from mundane bullets and em dashes to fancy fractions and ligatures—cannot be found on the keyboard. InDesign provides quick access to special characters in the Insert Special Character submenu in the Type menu and the Glyphs palette. (A *glyph* is a form of a character; for example, some fonts include several different versions of an ampersand. The smallest unit of a font is actually a glyph, not a character.) If you frequently access the same glyphs, you can save them as glyph sets.

## Inserting Common Special Characters

From the Insert Special Character submenu, you can insert commonly used characters such as a Bullet •, Copyright Symbol ©, Ellipsis ...,
Paragraph Symbol ¶, Registered Trademark Symbol ®, Em Dash —, or En Dash –. The character is inserted at the text insertion point and formatted with the active font. If you end up inserting these characters often, you might want to learn and remember their standard keyboard shortcuts or create your own (see #3). Applications such as KeyCaps can show you the keyboard shortcuts.

## Inserting Glyphs

To access every variation of every character within a font, choose Type > Glyphs to open the Glyphs palette (**Figure 36**). To insert a glyph at the text insertion point, scroll through the palette to locate it and then double-click it. The glyph is inserted and formatted according to the surrounding character formats.

The Glyphs palette provides access to all the fonts that are currently active on your system and contains a few options to choose from:

- **Font:** By default, the Glyphs palette displays the font in use at the text insertion point. You can select a different font from the menu in the lower-left corner of the palette. The menu next to it lets you choose a variation of the font such as Bold or Italic.

- **Scale:** Click the scale buttons ⬜ ⬜ in the lower-right corner of the palette to increase or decrease the size of the glyphs shown. This makes it easy to find the right glyph, but it does not affect the size of the character you insert.

- **Show:** You can narrow down the glyphs shown in the palette by choosing an option from the Show menu such as Alternates for Selection or Standard Ligatures. The options in this menu vary according to what the font vendor built into the font, with OpenType fonts generally offering the most options.

- **Alternates:** In OpenType fonts, some glyphs have *alternates*, or different visual forms, you can choose from. If you see an arrow in the lower-right corner of a glyph's field, click it to view and select alternates.

Figure 36 The Glyphs palette provides quick access to all the glyphs within the selected font. Double-click a glyph to insert it in text at the text insertion point.

## Saving Fonts with Glyphs

By default, when you add a glyph to a glyph set, InDesign associates the current font with it. This is useful for unusual glyphs that may not exist in every font. However, for more common glyphs, such as 1/2 fractions or bullets, you may not want to associate a font with each glyph. To save glyphs without font information, choose Edit Glyph Set from the Glyphs palette menu, and select the set you want to edit from the submenu. In the Edit Glyph Set dialog box, you can select a glyph and uncheck Remember Font with Glyph.

## Creating Glyph Sets

If you use certain glyphs frequently—for example, if you're working on a cookbook and need to access various fractions—you can save them as a glyph set for quick access. Glyph sets are saved with your copy of InDesign.

To create a glyph set:

1. Choose New Glyph Set from the Glyphs palette menu.

2. To add glyphs to the set, select a glyph and choose Add to Glyph Set from the palette menu. If you have more then one glyph set, select the appropriate set from the submenu.

3. To view glyphs in the set, choose the set from the Show menu at the top of the Glyphs palette.

As with other glyphs, you can insert a glyph from a set by double-clicking it.

# #**37** Anchoring Objects in Text

If you have pictures or other graphic elements that need to flow with related text, you can *anchor* the objects in the text. This prevents you from having to manually reposition objects such as charts, sidebars, or graphics every time text reflows. Any type of object can be anchored in text, including text frames, picture frames, paths, and tables. When you anchor objects, you can position them inline with text, above text, or in a custom position such as out in the margin (**Figure 37a**). You have precise control over object position, including the ability to fine-tune placement with the mouse.

**Figure 37a** Anchored objects flow with text. An Inline object (left) is positioned at the baseline of text at the text insertion point; an Above Line object is positioned above the line containing the text insertion point; a Custom object can be positioned outside the text frame, relative to the spine, margins, and more.

## Anchoring Existing Objects

You have two choices for anchoring objects: You can anchor existing objects or you can anchor placeholder objects. To anchor an existing object in text:

1. Select any type of object using one of the selection tools.

2. Choose Edit > Cut or Edit > Copy.

3. Select the Type tool and click in text to position the insertion point where you want the anchored object.

4. Choose Edit > Paste.

By default, the object is anchored inline, but you can reposition it using the Anchored Object Options dialog box. If the object is larger than surrounding text, it may overlap the text; in that case, you may need to adjust the leading or insert line breaks.

## Anchoring Placeholder Objects

If you haven't created the object that will be anchored—or if its content is not ready—you can create a rectangular placeholder and anchor it in text. To do this:

1. Select the Type tool and click in text to position the text insertion point.

2. Choose Object > Anchored Object > Insert.

3. In the Object Options area at the top of the Insert Anchored Object dialog box, specify the Content for the object (such as Text or Graphic).

4. Select an Object Style to base the object on (if you've created any).

5. Select a Paragraph Style for the text it will contain (if the object is a text frame).

6. Enter a Height and Width for the object.

You can also specify the position of the object, as discussed in the next section.

## Positioning Anchored Objects

To change the positioning of an anchored object, click it using a selection tool and choose Object > Anchored Object > Options. The controls in the Anchored Object Options dialog box are the same as those for positioning in the Insert Anchored Object dialog box. Choose an option from the Position menu at the top:

- **Inline or Above Line:** Select this option if you want to anchor the object inline with the text or above a line of text.

- **Custom:** Select this option if you want to anchor the object in a different position, such as out in the margin.

### Copying and Pasting Anchored Objects

Anchored objects and anchored object markers function just like characters when it comes to selecting, cutting, copying, and pasting them with the Type tool. If you need to copy and paste a story containing anchored graphics to a different location, for example, the graphics will come right along with it.

If you choose Inline or Above Line from the Position menu, the Anchored Object Options dialog box (**Figure 37b**) lets you specify which type of anchoring you want and then further fine-tune the positioning.

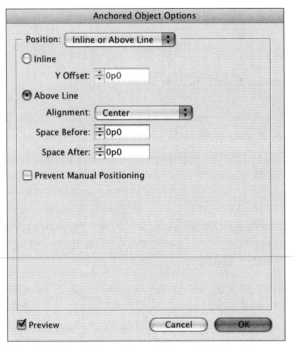

**Figure 37b** When Inline or Above Line is selected from the Position menu, the Anchored Object Options dialog box lets you specify the position of anchored objects that are flowing with or above lines of text.

- **Inline:** To position the object inline with text, click Inline. Enter a value in the Y Offset field to move the object up or down from the baseline of the text.

- **Above Line:** To position the object above the line containing the text insertion point, click Above Line. Choose an option from the Alignment menu to specify how the object is positioned within the text frame: Left, Center, Right, Towards Spine, Away from Spine, or Text Alignment (which matches the alignment of the paragraph). Enter values in the Space Before and Space After fields to control the amount of space above and below the anchored object.

If you choose Custom from the Position menu, the Anchored Object Options dialog box (**Figure 37c**) lets you specify precisely where the object should be placed.

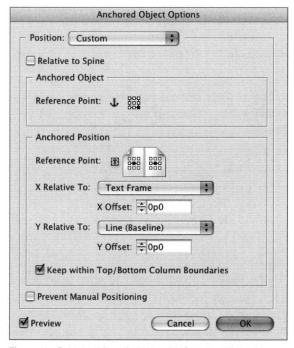

Figure 37c For an anchored object with Custom alignment, the Anchored Object Options dialog box lets you position it in relation to the columns of text, the page, and more.

- **Relative to Spine:** Check this option if you want the object's placement to be different for right-facing and left-facing pages. For example, if a book has a wide outer margin, you might place anchored objects in the margin. When text reflows from left to right pages, you'll want the anchored objects positioned accordingly.

- **Anchored Object Reference Point:** This option specifies what part of the anchored object should align with the page, text frame, or margins (as specified in the Anchored Object Position area below). For example, if the left edge of the object should align with the text frame, click a box on the left edge.

*(continued on next page)*

- **Anchored Object Position:** In this area, the X Relative To menu and X Offset field control the horizontal placement of the anchored object. The Y Relative To menu and Y Offset field control the vertical placement of the anchored object. The reference points available vary according to the selections you make in the X Relative To and Y Relative To fields, but essentially the Reference Point you click indicates the location on the page the object should align with.

The interplay of these settings is fairly complex, so be sure to check the Preview box so you can see any changes you make as you make them.

*Tip*

*In addition to all the positioning settings in the Anchored Object Options dialog box, you can drag anchored objects using the selection tools. If you're creating a template and don't want users to be able to move anchored items, check Prevent Manual Positioning.*

## Releasing Anchored Objects

If you no longer want an object to be anchored, select it with a selection tool. Then choose Object > Anchored Object > Release. (The Release command is available only for anchored objects with Custom alignment.) You can also copy and paste any selected anchored object to create an unanchored copy of it.

# #38 Wrapping Text Around Objects

The interplay of text and images in a layout contributes significantly to the overall message. You achieve a lot of this interplay by wrapping text around objects such as text frames or lines or around contours within a graphic such as a clipping path or alpha channel. You specify text wrap for the object that the text will wrap around. For example, if text will wrap around a picture frame, you specify text wrap for the picture frame. The object text wraps around is called the *wrap object* (**Figure 38a**).

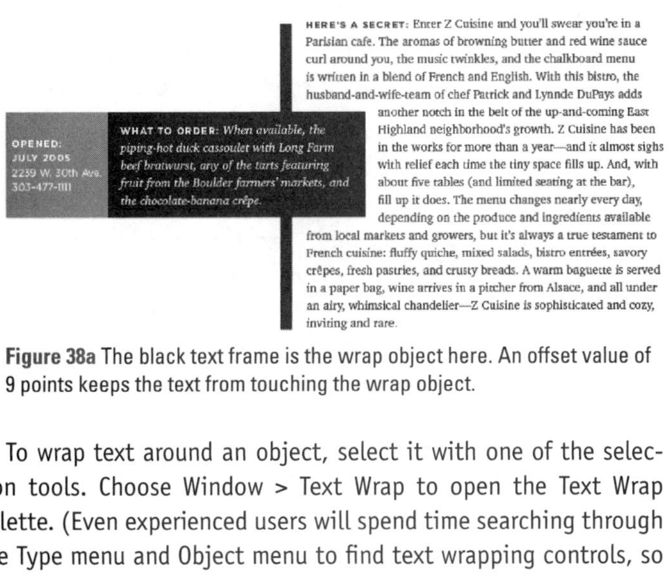

HERE'S A SECRET: Enter Z Cuisine and you'll swear you're in a Parisian cafe. The aromas of browning butter and red wine sauce curl around you, the music twinkles, and the chalkboard menu is written in a blend of French and English. With this bistro, the husband-and-wife-team of chef Patrick and Lynnde DuPays adds another notch in the belt of the up-and-coming East Highland neighborhood's growth. Z Cuisine has been in the works for more than a year—and it almost sighs with relief each time the tiny space fills up. And, with about five tables (and limited seating at the bar), fill up it does. The menu changes nearly every day, depending on the produce and ingredients available from local markets and growers, but it's always a true testament to French cuisine: fluffy quiche, mixed salads, bistro entrées, savory crêpes, fresh pastries, and crusty breads. A warm baguette is served in a paper bag, wine arrives in a pitcher from Alsace, and all under an airy, whimsical chandelier—Z Cuisine is sophisticated and cozy, inviting and rare.

OPENED: JULY 2005
2239 W. 30th Ave.
303-477-1111

WHAT TO ORDER: *When available, the piping-hot duck cassoulet with Long Farm beef bratwurst, any of the tarts featuring fruit from the Boulder farmers' markets, and the chocolate-banana crêpe.*

**Figure 38a** The black text frame is the wrap object here. An offset value of 9 points keeps the text from touching the wrap object.

To wrap text around an object, select it with one of the selection tools. Choose Window > Text Wrap to open the Text Wrap palette. (Even experienced users will spend time searching through the Type menu and Object menu to find text wrapping controls, so commit this one to memory—it's in the Window menu.) Once you find the Text Wrap palette (**Figure 38b**), using it is easy:

- **Wrap Shape buttons:** Click one of the first three buttons to indicate the shape of the text wrap—None 🔲, Bounding Box 🔲, or Object Shape 🔲. None places the object on top of text or flows text over the object. Bounding Box wraps text around the rectangular bounding box of the object, and Object Shape wraps text around the contours of the object.

- **Jump Object:** If you don't want text on either side of the object (only above or below it), click the Jump Object button 🔲.

*(continued on next page)*

## Flowing Text into Shapes

To flow text *into* a wrap object rather than around it, check Invert in the Text Wrap palette. For this to have any effect, the wrap object must be capable of containing text.

- **Jump to Next Column:** If you want text below the object to flow to the next column rather than under the object, click the Jump to Next Column button .

- **Offset fields:** Enter values in the fields to specify the amount of space between the wrap object and the text.

- **Contour Options:** If you want to wrap text around contours within a graphic, choose Show Options from the Text Wrap palette menu. The Type menu displays, but you need to click the Object Shape wrap button to enable it. You can then select from any alpha channels or Photoshop paths saved with the graphic file. If you've selected a clipping path for the graphic in the Clipping Path dialog box (Object menu), you can wrap text around it by choosing Same as Clipping. For a graphic with a lot of contrast between the foreground and background, you can use the Detect Edges option to create a text wrap contour.

- **Include Inside Edges:** If you're wrapping text around an image contour, you can flow text into any holes in the contour. For example, if you have a picture of a donut, you can flow text around the edges and into the white space in the center. To do this, check Include Inside Edges in the Contour Options area. (If the check box is not available, the selected contour has no holes.)

Once you have a text wrap specified, you can edit the contour using the Pen tool or the Direct Selection tool.

Figure 38b The Text Wrap palette lets you fine-tune the interplay of text and objects on the page.

### Note

*If you want to prevent text from wrapping around objects regardless of their text wrap settings, you can check Ignore Text Wrap for the text frame in the Text Frame Options dialog box (Object menu).*

# #**39** Applying Optical Margin Alignment

In typography, there is a difference between text that is actually aligned and text that is *optically aligned*. When text is left aligned or right aligned, the edges still look ragged sometimes due to the shape of the characters. For example, punctuation such as quotation marks, commas, and em dashes often cause this problem as do some letters such as "W" and "A." To fix this, InDesign provides *optical margin alignment*—also known as hanging punctuation— which "hangs" the edges of offending characters slightly outside the margins to produce a smoother looking edge (**Figure 39a**). This is a special effect that you will generally use sparingly for text such as pull quotes; it is not generally used for body text.

"The cutting board"
starter is a sampling
of rare Italian meats
and cheeses.
—We want to cater
to suits and baseball
caps, says Frizzi

"The cutting board"
starter is a sampling
of rare Italian meats
and cheeses.
—We want to cater to
suits and baseball caps,
says Frizzi

**Figure 39a** At left, the text is left aligned, but the left edge looks ragged due to the opening quotation marks and the em dash. At right, the text has optical margin alignment, so the quotation marks and em dash hang slightly outside the margin.

Optical Margin Alignment is an attribute of a story—which consists of all the text in a series of threaded text frames—so you cannot apply it to selected paragraphs. As a result, you may need to place text that requires Optical Margin Alignment in separate text frames. To apply Optical Margin Alignment:

1. Select a text frame with the Type tool or either selection tool.

2. Choose Type > Story.

*(continued on next page)*

**3.** Check Optical Margin Alignment in the Story palette (**Figure 39b**).

**4.** Specify how much the text should hang outside the margins by entering a point size in the field. In general, select the point size of the text itself.

**Figure 39b** Use the Story palette to create hanging punctuation for the selected text frame.

# #**40** Importing Tables from Word and Excel

In most workflows, data that will be presented in a table—whether it's financial data for an annual report or a price list for a catalog—is born in another program. It might be extracted from an accounting system and stored in a Microsoft Excel spreadsheet, or it might be a table a writer produced in Microsoft Word. Either way, InDesign makes it easy for you to handle tables created elsewhere: You import them like you import other text files. See #21 for more information about importing text.

### Note
*In InDesign, tables are always anchored in a text frame and always flow with surrounding text. For more information about anchored objects, see #37.*

## Importing Tables
To import tables from Word or Excel:

1. Choose File > Place.

2. In the Place dialog box, navigate to and select the Word (.doc) or Excel (.xls) file.

3. Check Show Import Options.

4. Click Open.

5. In the Formatting area in the Microsoft Word Import Options dialog box, make sure Preserve Formatting from Text and Tables is selected. In the Formatting area in the Microsoft Excel Import Options dialog box, make sure Formatted Table is selected from the Table menu (**Figure 40**).

6. Click OK.

7. Since the table is treated like text, the table is either imported at the text insertion point or the cursor is loaded and you click in an existing text frame or create a new one.

## Importing Unformatted Tables

Just because you can import formatted tables and spreadsheets from Word and Excel doesn't mean that you should. Given the formatting limitations of the software involved—and the possible design limitations of the people involved—you might just want to create and format the tables in InDesign. Generally, these programs and users are focused on more utilitarian purposes, such as making sure the numbers are all there and all correct. They are not likely to spend time making the tables attractive. You will probably end up reformatting all the text and the tables, and you may find that it's quicker and easier to just import unformatted text and convert it to tables. In a large project with many tables, you might want to experiment with a couple and decide how you want to handle them.

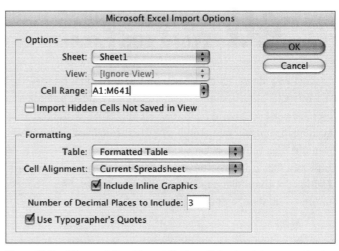

**Figure 40** The Microsoft Excel Import Options dialog box lets you customize how Excel tables are imported into InDesign.

## Linking Tables

When you import tables, spreadsheets, and text files, you have the option to link to the original file. If any changes occur in the original file, you can update the link in InDesign (using the Links palette) and the table or text is automatically updated. This is similar to updating the link to a graphic file, which InDesign maintains automatically. If you want to do this, check Create Links When Placing Text and Spreadsheet Files in the Type panel in the Preferences dialog box before you import the table. Then check the Links palette to see if a table needs to be updated. See #58 for more information about managing links.

Linking to tables sounds great, right? How many times do writers and accountants make changes after you have formatted their text and tables? But linking is really not as great as it seems, because if you update the link between InDesign and the original file, any formatting you applied in InDesign is lost. And why would you be using InDesign if not to make the table look better? Use this feature only if you're not planning to make formatting changes to the tables in InDesign.

# #41 Creating New Tables

If you need to build a table in InDesign from scratch, you can easily create one with the number of rows and columns you need. In addition, you can add header rows for labeling the table and footer rows for details and such. Since tables are always anchored in text, you need to click in a text frame to create a table. The table will automatically match the current column width, so if you need to create a text frame to contain a table, make it approximately the width you want for the table. (See #37 for more information about anchored objects.) To create a table:

1. Select the Type tool.

2. Click in a text frame to position the text insertion point wherever you want the table.

3. Choose Table > Insert Table.

4. In the Insert Table dialog box (**Figure 41a**), enter the number of horizontal rows you need for basic table data in the Body Rows field.

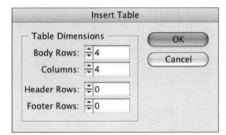

**Figure 41a**
The Insert Table dialog box lets you specify how many rows and columns you want in a new table.

5. Enter the number of vertical columns you need in the Columns field.

6. If you need header rows for the table (to contain a table head and column heads, for example), enter the number of rows in the Header Rows field.

*(continued on next page)*

**7.** If you need footer rows for the table (to contain a citation, for example), enter the number of rows in the Footer Rows field. The advantage to creating official Header Rows and Footer Rows is that they automatically repeat if the table splits across pages.

**8.** Click OK to create the table.

The table is anchored in text at the text insertion point. The height of the rows is based on the formatting of the text insertion point, whereas the width of the columns is calculated according to the width of the text frame and the number of columns requested (**Figure 41b**).

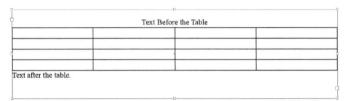

**Figure 41b** New tables are automatically anchored in surrounding text so if the text reflows, the table moves accordingly.

# #**42** Converting Text to Tables

The text that needs to go in a table often already exists, usually in a *tab-delimited format* (meaning that the cells of information for the table are separated by tabs). You do not need to retype this text into a new table; you can easily convert it into a table. To do this:

1. If necessary, import the text into a text frame.

2. Choose Type > Show Hidden Characters to determine how the text is currently separated (**Figure 42a**). Usually, you will see tabs between "columns" of information and paragraph returns between "rows" of information. Also, check to see that all the columns have the same amount of tabs between them; it doesn't matter if the tabs don't line up and the text looks messy. All that matters is consistency in the characters used.

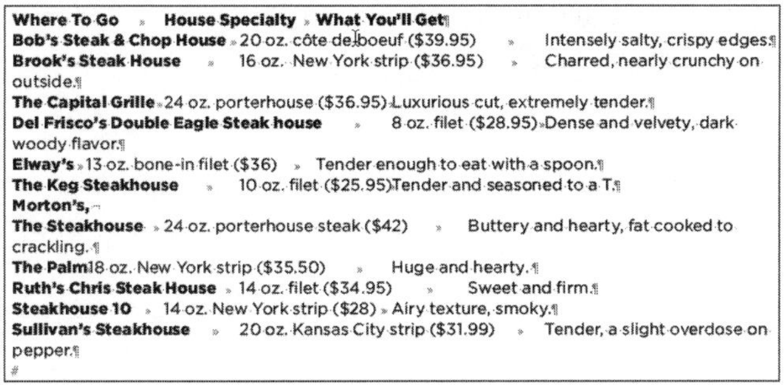

```
Where To Go    »   House Specialty  »  What You'll Get¶
Bob's Steak & Chop House » 20 oz. côte de boeuf ($39.95)      »    Intensely salty, crispy edges.¶
Brook's Steak House      »    16 oz. New York strip ($36.95)      »    Charred, nearly crunchy on
outside.¶
The Capital Grille » 24 oz. porterhouse ($36.95) » Luxurious cut, extremely tender.¶
Del Frisco's Double Eagle Steak house      »     8 oz. filet ($28.95) » Dense and velvety, dark
woody flavor.¶
Elway's » 13 oz. bone-in filet ($36)    »    Tender enough to eat with a spoon.¶
The Keg Steakhouse      »    10 oz. filet ($25.95) Tender and seasoned to a T.¶
Morton's, ¬
The Steakhouse  » 24 oz. porterhouse steak ($42)       Buttery and hearty, fat cooked to
crackling. ¶
The Palm 18 oz. New York strip ($35.50)     »    Huge and hearty. ¶
Ruth's Chris Steak House  » 14 oz. filet ($34.95)      »     Sweet and firm.¶
Steakhouse 10  »  14 oz. New York strip ($28) » Airy texture, smoky.¶
Sullivan's Steakhouse   »    20 oz. Kansas City strip ($31.99)    »    Tender, a slight overdose on
pepper.¶
#
```

Figure 42a Before converting text to a table, choose Type > Show Hidden Characters to determine what is separating columns (usually a tab) and what is separating rows (usually a paragraph return).

3. Select the Type tool and highlight the text to convert to a table.

4. Choose Table > Convert Text to Table.

*(continued on next page)*

**5.** In the Convert Text to Table dialog box (**Figure 42b**), confirm the information selected for the Column Separator and Row Separator. If necessary, you can change the separators by choosing Tab, Comma, or Paragraph from the menus or by entering a different separation character (such as a semicolon) in the fields.

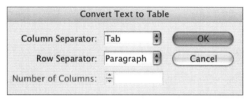

**Figure 42b** The Convert Text to Table dialog box lets you specify the characters used to separate columns and rows in the text.

**6.** If you choose the same separation character for columns and rows, you can clarify how many columns you need by entering a value in the Number of Columns field. Otherwise, this field is unavailable.

**7.** Click OK to create the table.

You may need to manually adjust the column widths as we did (**Figure 42c**), and you can add header and footer rows as necessary.

| Where To Go | House Specialty | What You'll Get |
|---|---|---|
| **Bob's Steak & Chop House** | 20 oz. côte de boeuf ($39.95) | Intensely salty, crispy edges. |
| **Brook's Steak House** | 16 oz. New York strip ($36.95) | Charred, nearly crunchy on outside. |
| **The Capital Grille** | 24 oz. porterhouse ($36.95) | Luxurious cut, extremely tender. |
| **Del Frisco's Double Eagle Steak house** | 8 oz. filet ($28.95) | Dense and velvety, dark woody flavor. |
| **Elway's** | 13 oz. bone-in filet ($36) | Tender enough to eat with a spoon. |
| **The Keg Steakhouse** | 10 oz. filet ($25.95) | Tender and seasoned to a T. |
| **Morton's, The Steakhouse** | 24 oz. porterhouse steak ($42) | Buttery and hearty, fat cooked to crackling. |
| **The Palm** | 18 oz. New York strip ($35.50) | Huge and hearty. |
| **Ruth's Chris Steak House** | 14 oz. filet ($34.95) | Sweet and firm. |
| **Steakhouse 10** | 14 oz. New York strip ($28) | Airy texture, smoky. |
| **Sullivan's Steakhouse** | 20 oz. Kansas City strip ($31.99) | Tender, a slight overdose on pepper. |

**Figure 42c** InDesign converts the highlighted text to a table, but it's likely that you'll have to adjust the column widths based on the content.

# #43 Adding Content to Tables

Tables consist of individual cells, which are actually miniature text frames. You can enter text in individual cells, or you can anchor graphics in them. The one thing you cannot do is flow text through table cells as if they were threaded. If text already exists that you'd like to flow through a table, you're better off converting it to a table (see #42).

## Adding Text to Tables

To add text to a table cell, click in the cell with the Type tool. You can then type in that cell, paste text into the cell (Edit > Paste), or import text into the cell (File > Place). To navigate between cells, press the Tab key to jump to the next cell and press Shift+Tab to jump to the previous cell. Row height will adjust automatically to accommodate the amount of text you type in the cell.

## Adding Graphics to Tables

Since table cells are just small text frames, to place graphics in them you anchor the graphic in text. With tables, it's easiest to size the graphic appropriately first, before you anchor it. That way, you know the graphic will fit in the cell. To anchor a graphic in text, select it with the Selection tool and choose Edit > Cut. Select the Type tool, click in a cell where you want the graphic, and choose Edit > Paste (**Figure 43**). You can also click in a cell and choose Object > Anchored Object > Insert to anchor a placeholder for a graphic.

**Figure 43** You can combine text and graphics in the same table cell by simply anchoring a graphic in text like the steak shown here.

# #44 Formatting Tables

With the table formatting options, you can create eye-catching, easy-to-read tables by automatically applying strokes and fills to alternating rows or columns of information, specifying different strokes and fills for individual cells, applying a border to the entire table, and much more. To access the formatting controls, you need to select all or parts of a table with the Type tool. All the formatting commands are available in the Table menu and the Table palette menu (Window > Type & Tables > Table).

## Formatting the Entire Table

To format an entire table as opposed to individual cells, click in the table with the Type tool to select it. Then choose Table > Table Options > Table Setup. The Table Setup panel (**Figure 44a**) lets you change the number of rows and columns, add a table border, and specify the amount of space before and after the table. The Row Strokes, Column Strokes, and Fills panels let you apply a pattern of strokes and/or fills such as applying a fill to every third column.

> **Tip**
> *To position the table within the text frame that it's anchored in, select the paragraph the table is anchored in and click one of the alignment buttons in the Paragraph panel in the Control palette.*

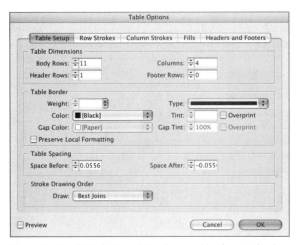

**Figure 44a** The Table Options dialog box provides formats for the entire table such as a table border and alternating row strokes.

## Formatting Cells

To format cells, you first need to make a selection—a single cell, multiple adjacent cells, or the entire table. You can then specify how the text is positioned within the cell, specify strokes and fills for the cell, and even highlight cells with a pattern of diagonal lines. To make a selection, use the Type tool and then do one of the following:

- Click in a single cell to select it.
- Click and drag to select multiple cells.
- Click outside the table when the arrow pointer displays. This lets you select entire rows or columns.
- Choose an option from the Table > Select submenu, including Cell, Row, Column, or Table.

Once you have cells selected to format, choose Table > Cell Options > Text. The Text panel in the Cell Options dialog box (**Figure 44b**) lets you change text inset, vertical justification, first baseline, and rotation of text within the cells. The Strokes and Fills, Rows and Columns, and Diagonal Lines panels let you specify cell sizes and add strokes and/or fills to the cells for emphasis or clarity.

**Figure 44b** The Cell Options dialog box lets you specify the text placement, strokes, and fills for selected cells.

**#44**: Formatting Tables

### Formatting Text in Tables

To format text in tables, select the text with the Type tool as always. To select entire rows or columns, click outside the table when the arrow pointer displays. Use the standard text formatting controls: the Character and Paragraph panels in the Control palette, the Character and Paragraph palettes (Type menu), and the Character Styles and Paragraph Styles palettes (Type menu).

## Using the Table Palette

The table formatting options you use the most are also available in the Table palette (**Figure 44c**). To open the palette, choose Window > Type & Tables > Table. Point at the controls on the palette to display their Tool Tips and see what they do. The Table palette menu provides quick access to most of the commands in the Table menu.

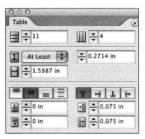

**Figure 44c** The Table palette provides quick access to commonly used table formatting options such as number of rows and columns, and text inset within cells.

# #45 Adding Headers and Footers to Tables

For a table to be useful, it generally needs row and column headings—so you know what information is in them. This is easy to accomplish with a row at the top of the table containing column headings and a column down the left containing row heads. A problem occurs, however, if the table is split across several columns, text frames, or pages. The column heads become separated from their columns, leaving the reader to guess what's in them. Fortunately, InDesign provides a simple solution with its header rows feature that automatically repeats the necessary rows whenever the table splits. In addition, if you need a footer in the table (to contain a disclaimer or source, for example), footer rows can repeat as well.

In the sample table (**Figure 45a**), the first row is designated as a header. So if we add 20 more steakhouses and need to continue the table on another page, the column heads will repeat. The last row is designated as a footer, so it will repeat as well.

| Where To Go | House Specialty | What You'll Get |
|---|---|---|
| Bob's Steak & Chop House | 20 oz. côte de boeuf ($39.95) | Intensely salty, crispy edges. |
| Brook's Steak House | 16 oz. New York strip ($36.95) | Charred, nearly crunchy on outside. |
| The Capital Grille | 24 oz. porterhouse ($36.95) | Luxurious cut, extremely tender. |
| Del Frisco's Double Eagle Steak house | 8 oz. filet ($28.95) | Dense and velvety, dark woody flavor. |
| Elway's | 13 oz. bone-in filet ($36) | Tender enough to eat with a spoon. |
| The Keg Steakhouse | 10 oz. filet ($25.95) | Tender and seasoned to a T. |
| Morton's, The Steakhouse | 24 oz. porterhouse steak ($42) | Buttery and hearty, fat cooked to crackling. |
| The Palm | 18 oz. New York strip ($35.50) | Huge and hearty. |
| Ruth's Chris Steak House | 14 oz. filet ($34.95) | Sweet and firm. |
| Steakhouse 10 | 14 oz. New York strip ($28) | Airy texture, smoky. |
| Sullivan's Steakhouse | 20 oz. Kansas City strip ($31.99) | Tender, a slight overdose on pepper. |
| Visited in Fall 2005; prices and menus may vary. | | |

**Figure 45a** In this table, the first row is a header and the last row is a footer. These rows will repeat as necessary if the table flows across pages.

## Creating Header and Footer Rows

You have two choices for creating header and footer rows: You can convert existing rows, or you can add new rows.

- **Converting Rows:** If you realize that a table needs to continue in a different column, text frame, or page after you've created and formatted the entire table, you can convert the rows containing the header and footer information into actual header and footer rows. To do this, select the rows containing the header or footer information. (Using the Type tool, click outside the table when the arrow pointer displays.) Choose Table > Convert Rows > To Header or Table > Convert Rows > To Footer. If you're using both headers and footers in a table, you'll have to convert the rows separately.

- **Adding New Rows:** To add new rows for headers and footers, choose Table > Table Options > Headers and Footers. In the Headers and Footers panel (**Figure 45b**), enter the number of header rows to add in the Header Rows field. Enter the number of footer rows to add in the Footer Rows field.

- **Headers and Footers Options:** Whether you convert existing rows or add new headers and footers, you can control how often they appear in the Headers and Footers panel. Use the Repeat menus to specify whether the row should appear every time the table flows to a new column, to a new text frame, or only to a new page. If the start of the table contains column headings or footer information in a different format, such as a graphic, you can remove the header and footer from the start of the table. To do this, click Skip First in the Header area and/or the Footer area.

If you change your mind about header and footer rows, you can select the rows and delete them or decrease the number of Header Rows or Footer Rows in the Headers and Footers panel.

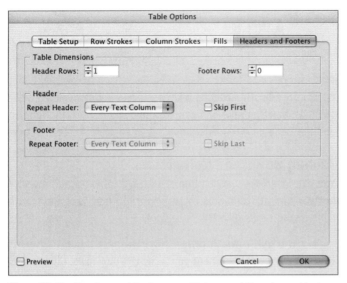

**Figure 45b** The Headers and Footers panel lets you add header and footer rows to the selected table and control how often the rows repeat.

## Editing Header and Footer Text

When you edit content in rows designated as headers and footers, the text and graphics automatically update wherever the header and footer is used. (As a result, do not insert words such as "continued" in the header of the continuation of a table because it will show up on the first part of the table as well.) To quickly jump to a header and footer row to start editing it, choose Table > Edit Header or Table > Edit Footer.

# #46 Editing Tables

When it comes to tables, change is inevitable. You will find yourself constantly adjusting column widths and row heights, adding rows and columns, deleting rows and columns, and so on. Both the Table menu and the Table palette menu provide many options for editing tables.

## Adding Rows and Columns

You can insert rows and columns within a table, or add rows to the bottom and add columns to the right. To add rows and columns, click in the table with the Type tool.

- **Inserting rows:** To insert rows within a table, click in a row above or below where you want the new rows. Choose Table > Insert > Row. In the Insert Rows(s) dialog box (**Figure 46a**), enter the number of rows to insert in the Number field and then click Above or Below to indicate the position.

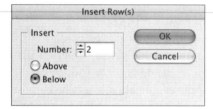

Figure 46a The Insert Row(s) dialog box lets you specify how many rows to insert and where to insert them.

- **Inserting columns:** To insert columns within a table, click in a column to the left or right of where you want the new columns. Choose Table > Insert > Column. In the Insert Column(s) dialog box, enter the number of columns to insert in the Number field and then click Left or Right to indicate the position.

- **Adding rows or columns:** To add rows or columns on to the table, change the values in the Body Rows field or the Columns field in the Table Setup panel (Table > Options > Table Setup). You can also change the values in the Number of Rows field or the Number of Columns field in the Table palette (Window > Type & Tables > Table). New rows are added to the bottom of the table, and new columns are added to the right side of the table. (A quick way to add a row to the bottom of a table is to press Tab when the insertion point is in the last cell in the table.)

## Deleting Rows, Columns, and Tables

The Delete key will eliminate just about any selection in InDesign—selected text and objects, for example. It will not, however, delete selections within a table but will delete the contents instead.

To delete parts of a table or a table, make a selection first. With the Type tool, click in a row, column, or table that you want to delete. Choose Table > Select, and then choose Row, Column, or Table. You can also click outside the table when the arrow pointer displays to select a row or column (**Figure 46b**). Drag the arrow pointer to select multiple rows or columns. Once you've made a selection, choose Table > Delete, and then choose Row, Column, or Table.

### Note
*If you decrease the number of rows or columns in fields in the Table Setup panel or the Table palette, rows will be deleted from the bottom of the table and columns will be deleted from the right side of the table.*

Figure 46b When you point outside a table with the Type tool, the arrow pointer lets you select entire rows and columns.

**Merging Cells**

If you want to combine multiple cells in a row or column into a single cell, select the cells and choose Table > Merge Cells.

# Resizing Tables, Rows, and Columns

If the initial column widths and row heights are not quite right—and they rarely are—they are easy to adjust. Using the Type tool, you can drag the gridlines between rows and columns to adjust the sizes (**Figure 46c**). You can also drag any edge of the table to resize the table height or width in any given direction.

To "clean up" a table so the columns are the same width and the rows are the same height, choose Table > Distribute Columns Evenly or Table > Distribute Rows Evenly. You can also specify a height for selected rows and a width for selected columns in the Table palette and in the Rows and Columns panel in the Cell Options dialog box (Table menu).

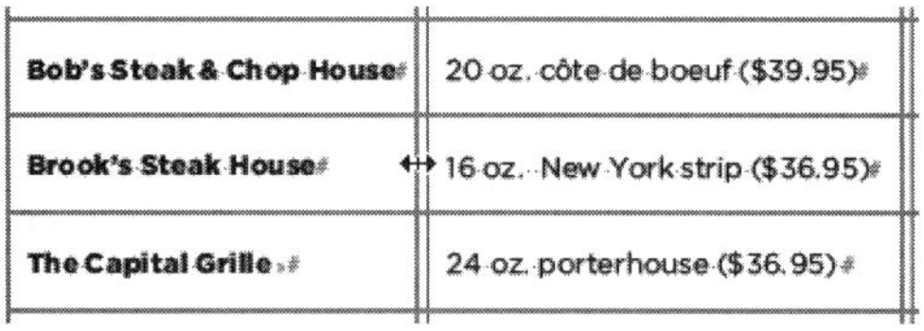

| Bob's Steak & Chop House | 20 oz. côte de boeuf ($39.95) |
| Brook's Steak House | 16 oz. New York strip ($36.95) |
| The Capital Grille | 24 oz. porterhouse ($36.95) |

**Figure 46c** Using the Type tool, drag the gridlines to adjust column width and row heights.

# CHAPTER FIVE

# Drawing Lines and Shapes

Although InDesign is not a dedicated illustration program like its close cousin, Illustrator, it includes several drawing tools and illustration features that can create virtually any kind of line or shape you can imagine. You can use the lines and shapes you create as graphic elements, as containers for text and graphics, and as paths along which text flows.

In this chapter, you'll start by learning how to use the Line and Pencil tools to draw relatively simple lines. Next, you'll learn how to use the Pen tool to create complex lines and shapes. Then you'll move on to drawing basic shapes with the Rectangle, Ellipse, and Polygon tools. And finally we'll show you how to create more complex shapes using the Pathfinder palette and other InDesign drawing features.

# #**47** Drawing Simple Lines

Before we take a look at InDesign's drawing tools, it's worth noting that InDesign doesn't distinguish between open and closed shapes, which are collectively referred to as *paths*. You can use any path as a graphic element or as a frame to hold text or a graphic, and you can flow text along any path. For example, you can draw a wavy line with the Pen tool and then:

- Add a stroke and a fill

- Place text or a graphic within it

- Flow text along it

If a layout requires a straight line of any kind, the Line tool offers the easiest way to create it. Select the Line tool, and then click and drag on a page or the pasteboard (**Figure 47a**). The point where you click is one end of the line; the point where you release the mouse button is the other end. As you drag, InDesign displays a line between the start and end points and its midpoint. If you hold down the Shift key as you drag, the angle of the line is restricted to increments of 45°.

**Figure 47a** Click and drag with the Line tool to create a straight line.

Creating straight lines is a cinch. Creating curvy lines is another matter. One option is to use the Pencil tool, which lets you use the mouse as a pencil; the other option is the Pen tool, which lets you create complex paths but is not particularly easy to use. (See #48 for more about using the Pen tool.) To use the Pencil tool, select it, and then click and drag the mouse as if it were a pencil (**Figure 47b**). You'll quickly learn that a mouse is not a very good pencil. If you need more control than the mouse offers, you might want to consider purchasing a graphic tablet.

If you want to create a closed path with the Pencil tool, begin dragging and then hold down Option (Mac OS) or Alt (Windows) as you drag. To close the path, make sure you release the mouse button before you release the Alt or Option key.

**Figure 47b** The Pencil tool lets you create freeform lines. This example was created using a graphics tablet, which is easier to use than a mouse for creating freeform shapes.

After you create a line, use the Selection tool to select and move it or to resize it by dragging a bounding box handle. Use the Direct Selection tool to move either of the endpoints of a straight line or any of the anchor points of a line created with the Pencil tool.

You can modify lines in many ways. For example, you can assign a stroke weight and style, and apply a color and tint. You can rotate, shear, and flip lines, and so on. (For more about modifying lines and other objects, see Chapter 7, "Working with Objects.")

## Setting Defaults for the Drawing Tools

By default, the Basic Graphics Frame object style is applied to objects you create with the Line, Pencil, and Pen tools, as well as the Rectangle, Ellipse, and Polygon tools (but not the Rectangle Frame, Ellipse Frame, and Polygon Frame tools and the Type tool). Unless you modify it, the Basic Graphics Frame object style produces objects with a 1-point stroke and no fill. The Rectangle Frame, Ellipse Frame, and Polygon Frame tools always create objects with no fill and no stroke.

To change the default settings used by the Line, Pencil, Pen, Rectangle, Ellipse, and Polygon tools you can modify the Basic Graphics Frame style when no objects are selected, assign a different object style to the tools, or change any object-related settings (such as stroke, fill, drop shadow, or blending mode) when no objects are selected. (For more about using object styles, see #67.)

By default, the Basic Text Frame object style is applied to text frames you create with the Type tool. The easiest way to change the appearance of text frames created with the Type tool is to modify the Basic Text Frame object style when nothing is selected.

#47: Drawing Simple Lines

# #48 Drawing Complex Lines

Most page layout and graphic programs have a drawing tool that's similar to InDesign's Pen tool. These tools let you create Bézier curves (also known as vector shapes), which are mathematically defined line segments. Bézier curves can be formed into complex paths that have straight edges, curved edges, or both.

If you're an Illustrator user or you've used Beziér tools in other programs, you'll be immediately comfortable with InDesign's Pen tool. If you've never used a tool like the Pen tool, it will probably take a little time for you to get comfortable with it.

Here's an easy way to get started with the Pen tool:

1. Select it in the toolbox.

2. Click an empty area of a page or the pasteboard and release the mouse button.

3. Move the Pen pointer, and then click and release the mouse button again.

4. To create additional straight segments, continue moving the pointer, and then click and release the mouse (**Figure 48a**).

5. To create an open path with two endpoints, select another tool when you're done creating segments. To create a closed path, move the pointer back to the first point you created, and then click the mouse when a small white circle is displayed next to the Pen pointer.

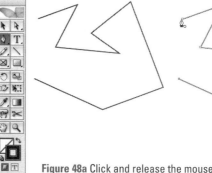

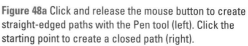

**Figure 48a** Click and release the mouse button to create straight-edged paths with the Pen tool (left). Click the starting point to create a closed path (right).

Creating a path that's made up of curved lines is a little different than creating straight-edged paths. Instead of clicking and releasing the mouse button when using the Pen tool, click and drag about one-third of the distance to the next anchor point before releasing the mouse.

When you click and drag with the Pen tool, InDesign creates an anchor point and a pair of opposing direction lines that form a straight line and meet at the anchor point. A curved segment is drawn to the preceding anchor point (**Figure 48b**). Continue clicking and dragging to create additional points and curved segments. Choose a different tool or click the starting point to complete the object.

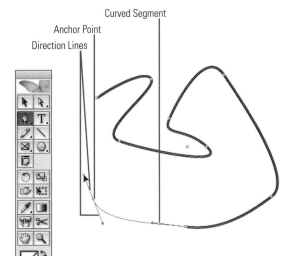

**Figure 48b** Click and drag the mouse in the direction of the next anchor point to create curved lines and shapes. This example shows the anchor points along a curved path. The anchor point that ends the path is selected, and you can see the direction lines that are displayed while clicking and dragging.

By combining the click-and-release method for creating straight segments and the click-and-drag method for creating curved segments, you can use the Pen tool to create paths that have both straight edges and curved edges.

If you're not satisfied with the results after using the Pen tool, it's easy to modify your creation. Use the Direct Selection tool to select and move anchor points and their accompanying direction lines. You can also use the Direct Selection tool to click and drag a segment of a path, and you can click and drag an object's center point to move the object. Use the Selection tool to move the object or to resize its bounding box.

The tools that are grouped with the Pen tool in the toolbox also let you modify paths:

**Add Anchor Point tool:** Click a path with the Add Anchor Point tool to add an anchor point.

**Delete Anchor Point tool:** Click an anchor point with the Delete Anchor Point tool to remove an anchor point.

**Convert Direction Point tool:** Click a corner anchor point with the Convert Direction Point tool, and then drag to convert it to a smooth anchor point.

By default, the Pen tool adds a 1-point stroke and no fill to the paths you create with it. To change the default settings for the Pen tool, modify the settings of the Basic Graphics Frame object style, choose a different object style from the Object Style menu in the Control palette when no objects are selected, or change object attributes such as fill color and tint, stroke weight and style, and so on, when no objects are selected.

# #49 Drawing Basic Shapes

The Rectangle, Ellipse, and Polygon tools, and their next-door neighbors, the Rectangle Frame, Ellipse Frame, and Polygon Frame tools, let you create closed shapes that you can use as graphic elements, containers for text and graphics, and paths along which text flows.

The Rectangle, Ellipse, and Polygon tools let you create "unassigned" frames, that is, frames that don't contain anything, whereas the three frame tools let you create graphics frames into which you can import graphics. (You can tell the difference between an unassigned frame and an empty graphics frame by the X that's displayed within the graphics frame.) Because it's easy to change the content of an empty frame, it doesn't matter whether you use the Rectangle, Ellipse, or Polygon tools or the corresponding frame tools (Rectangle Frame, Ellipse Frame, or Polygon frame) to create basic shapes.

To create a basic shape, select the appropriate tool, and then click and drag (**Figure 49**).

## Setting Defaults for the Polygon Tool

To set defaults for the Polygon tool or the Polygon Frame tool, double-click the tool in the toolbox. The Polygon Settings dialog box lets you specify the number of sides and, optionally, a star inset, which creates a starburst shape. The settings you specify are used for new polygons until you change settings again.

**Figure 49** Click and drag the mouse to create a basic shape. In this example, the Polygon tool is selected. Holding down the Shift key while dragging creates a polygon with equal sides and angles.

## Changing the Content Type of an Empty Frame

InDesign lets you create three types of frames: text frames (with the Type tool), graphics frames (with the Rectangle Frame, Ellipse Frame, and Polygon Frame tools), and unassigned frames (with the Rectangle, Ellipse, and Polygon tools). You can change the content type for an empty frame by selecting it, choosing Object > Content, and then making a selection from the submenu (Graphic, Text, or Unassigned).

## Using the Type Tool to Create Text Frames

Click and drag with the Type tool to create a new rectangular text frame. You can also use the Rectangle or Rectangle Frame tool, and then click within the frame with the Type tool. Hold down the Shift key as you drag to create a square frame. If you need to create a text frame within a text frame, use the Rectangle or Rectangle Frame tool to create the inner frame, and then click within the frame with the Type tool.

- The Rectangle and Rectangle Frame tools let you create rectangles and squares. Hold down the Shift key when dragging to create a square.

- The Ellipse and Ellipse Frame tools let you create ellipses and circles. Hold down the Shift key when dragging to create a circle.

- The Polygon and Polygon Frame tools let you create equal-sided polygons and starburst shapes. Hold down the Shift key to create a polygon with equal sides and angles. Press the up arrow key as you drag to add sides to the polygon you're creating; press the down arrow key to subtract sides. Press the right arrow key as you drag to increase the star inset in 10% increments; press the left arrow key as you drag to decrease the star inset in 10% increments. Press and hold while dragging to continually add or delete points or increase or decrease the star inset. (When a star inset is specified, the polygon tool creates a starburst shape instead of a regular polygon.)

In addition to the click-and-drag method of drawing basic shapes, you can also click once on a page or the pasteboard when any of the drawing tools is selected. When you click, a dialog box lets you specify height and width of the shape.

# #50 Creating Complex Shapes

While the Pen tool is the only tool that lets you *draw* complex shapes, InDesign offers a handy palette that lets you *create* complex shapes from two or more basic shapes. When multiple objects are selected, the Pathfinder palette (Window > Object & Layout > Pathfinder) provides five options for creating a single shape that's generated from the selected objects. The results you get from the Pathfinder options depend on the stacking order of the selected objects. If you don't get the results you want, use the Arrange commands (Object > Arrange) to adjust the stacking order.

Here's a brief explanation of the Pathfinder options:

**Add:** Combines the selected objects to form a single, all encompassing shape (**Figure 50a**).

**Subtract:** All objects in front of the backmost object are removed (**Figure 50b**).

**Intersect:** Creates a shape from overlapping areas and excludes areas that don't overlap (**Figure 50c**).

**Exclude Overlap:** The opposite of Intersect. Creates a shape from areas that do not overlap (**Figure 50d**).

**Minus Back:** Somewhat like Subtract. All objects in back of the frontmost object are removed (**Figure 50e**).

The five Pathfinder options are also available as commands in the Object menu (Object > Pathfinder).

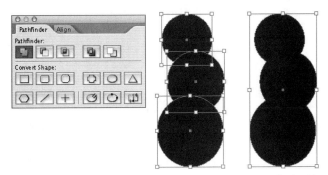

**Figure 50a** The Add button combines multiple objects into a single object.

## If You Can't Draw It Easily with InDesign ...

InDesign's drawing features are capable of handling many illustration tasks, but if your drawing requirements exceed InDesign's capabilities, your best bet is to use a dedicated illustration program, like Illustrator. You can even begin work on an illustration in Illustrator, and then copy and paste it into InDesign and use InDesign's drawing features to further modify the illustration.

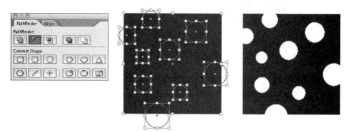

**Figure 50b** In this example, the Subtract option in the Pathfinder palette generated the shape on the right by "punching out" several circles from a square black background frame (center).

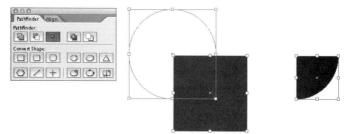

**Figure 50c** The Intersect button creates an object from overlapping areas.

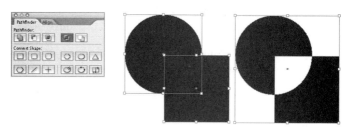

**Figure 50d** The Exclude Overlap button creates an object from areas that don't overlap.

**Figure 50e** The Minus Back button removes the background objects from the frontmost object.

# #51 Converting Shapes

If you need to make minor modifications to an object's shape, select it with the Direct Selection tool, and then move anchor points, direction points, and segments. For bigger modifications, use the Add Anchor Point, Delete Anchor Point, and Convert Direction Point tools, which are grouped with the Pen tool in the toolbox. To convert an object into one of 12 predefined shapes, use the Pathfinder palette (Window > Object & Layout > Pathfinder).

To change an object's shape with the Pathfinder palette, select the object, and then click one of the nine convert shape buttons in the palette (**Figure 51**):

- **Rectangle**
- **Rounded Corner Rectangle**
- **Beveled Corner Rectangle**
- **Inverse Rounded Corner Rectangle**
- **Ellipse**
- **Triangle**
- **Polygon**
- **Line**
- **Vertical/Horizontal Line**

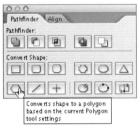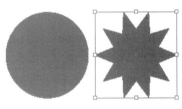

**Figure 51** Click one of the convert shape buttons in the Pathfinder palette to change the shape of the selected object. In this example, the circle was converted to a polygon. When you convert a shape to a polygon, the current settings of the Polygon tool are used.

## Using the Scissors Tool

You can use the Scissors tool to convert a closed shape to an open shape and to cut an open shape into two pieces. To use the Scissors tool, select it in the toolbox, and then move the crosshair pointer over the edge of an object. When a circle is displayed in the middle of the crosshairs—indicating that the pointer is over the edge of the object—click the mouse button. An anchor point is displayed where you click. If you select this anchor point with the Direct Selection tool and move it, you'll find another anchor point in the same place. This anchor point is the other endpoint if you cut a closed path. It's an endpoint on a separate path if you cut an open path.

You'll find three additional buttons for changing the shape of objects at the bottom right of the Pathfinder palette:

- **Open Path button:** The Open Path button creates an open shape from a closed shape, much like using the Scissors tool on a closed shape. InDesign chooses an anchor point at which the shape is opened. You may need to select the object with the Direct Selection tool to determine where the object has been split.

- **Close Path button:** The Close Path button creates a closed shape from an open shape by connecting the two endpoints.

- **Reverse Path button:** If you've created a shape with one or more "holes" in it—for example, a donut shape created by using the Subtract button on a pair of concentric circles—selecting the inner path and then clicking the Reverse Path button in the Pathfinder palette will eliminate the hole while keeping the path. Clicking the Reverse Path button again will show the hole.

# CHAPTER SIX

# Working with Graphics

In addition to using InDesign's drawing tools to create graphic elements within InDesign, you can also import graphics created with other programs. After you import a graphic into an InDesign layout, you can modify it in many ways, such as cropping, scaling, rotating, or flipping it horizontally or vertically. You can also use InDesign to apply see-through effects to imported graphics that make them appear translucent.

In this chapter we begin by explaining how to import graphics into InDesign layouts, and then tell you how to use some of InDesign's most powerful features to modify imported graphics and manage the graphic files.

# #52 Placing Graphics

InDesign lets you import a broad range of common graphic formats, including TIFF, JPEG, PDF, and EPS, as well as several lesser-known formats like DCS, PNG, and Scitex CT. You can also import native Photoshop and Illustrator files. Once you import a graphic into a layout, InDesign lets you modify it in several ways, as explained in #53, #54, and #55.

To place a graphic into an InDesign document, simply choose File > Place. (Unlike other popular page layout programs, InDesign doesn't require you to create a frame before you import a graphic, although you can work this way in InDesign if you want to.) The Place dialog box (**Figure 52**) lets you locate and choose the graphic. What happens after you click Open depends on what object, if any, is selected.

## Changing Your Mind After Importing a Graphic

If you click the Open button in the Place dialog box and then discover that you've inadvertently placed a graphic into the wrong frame, press Cmd+Z (Mac OS) or Ctrl+Z (Windows). The loaded graphics icon is displayed, and you can click within an empty frame, click an empty area on the page or pasteboard to create a new graphics frame that's the same size as the graphic, or click and drag to create a new custom-sized graphics frame.

**Figure 52** The Place dialog box lets you select the graphic you want to place into an InDesign layout. If you select Show Import Options, another dialog box is displayed after you click Open and offers several options for controlling the display of the graphic.

- If nothing is selected, the loaded graphics icon ⬚ is displayed, and you can click once or click and drag to place the graphic into a new graphics frame. If you just click, the frame is the same size as the graphic. If you click and drag, the rectangle you create becomes the frame for the graphic. You can also click within an empty frame to place the graphic within it.

- If a graphics or unassigned frame is selected, the graphic is placed within the frame.

- If the text insertion cursor is flashing, the graphic is placed within the text frame as an anchored graphic. An anchored graphic is treated like a text character and moves when editing causes text to reflow.

After you import a graphic into an InDesign layout, InDesign maintains a link between the graphic file and the InDesign document. InDesign uses the original graphic file to display it at high resolution, and the original graphic files are also used when you print or export an InDesign document that contains imported graphics. The Links palette (Window > Links) displays a list of all placed graphics. For information about managing links to graphic files, see #58.

### Dragging and Dropping Graphics

In addition to using the Place command (File menu) to import graphics, you can drag and drop graphic files into InDesign layouts. To drag and drop a graphic, click a graphic file in the Mac OS Finder, Windows Explorer, the desktop, or Adobe Bridge, drag the file icon into an InDesign document window, and then release the mouse button.

# #**53** Cropping and Resizing Graphics

After you import a graphic, chances are you'll want to resize it, crop it, or both. InDesign offers several ways to scale and crop imported graphics. But before you begin working with graphics, it's important to understand some basics about how InDesign handles them.

Every imported graphic is contained within a graphics frame. Most graphics frames are rectangular; however, you can use any object (except a text frame) as a graphics frame regardless of its shape.

Use the Selection tool to select a graphic and its frame, or use the Direct Selection tool or the Position tool, which is paired with the Direct Selection tool in the toolbox, to select only the graphic (**Figure 53a**). If you look closely, you'll notice that the bounding box of a selected graphics frame is displayed in a different color than the border around a selected graphic. Once you select a graphics frame or graphic, you're ready to modify the selection.

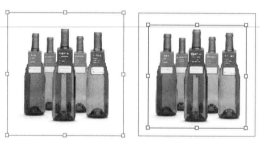

**Figure 53a** A graphics frame selected with the Selection tool (left). A graphic within a graphics frame selected with the Direct Selection tool (right).

You can show and hide different portions of a graphic by adjusting the size and shape of its frame or by adjusting the size of the graphic. The Selection tool is the best tool for cropping graphics. To crop a graphic by resizing its frame:

1. Choose the Selection tool, and then click on or within a graphics frame.

2. Drag any of the eight resizing handles to control what portion of the graphic is visible. If the frame is an irregular shape, use the Selection tool to resize its bounding box or use the Direct Selection tool to drag anchor points or segments and change the shape of the frame.

You can resize a graphic and its frame at the same time manually or by specifying scale percentages. To resize a graphic and its frame manually:

1. Select the frame with the Selection tool.

2. Hold down the Shift and Ctrl keys (Windows) or the Shift and Cmd keys (Mac OS), and drag a handle. If you hold down only the Ctrl key or the Cmd key as you drag, the frame and graphic are scaled disproportionately. If you hold down only the Shift key, the frame is scaled proportionally and the scale of the graphic does not change.

To resize a graphic and its frame by specifying scale percentages:

1. Select the frame with the Selection tool.

2. Enter values in the Scale X Percentage or Scale Y Percentage fields in the Transform palette or the Control palette. If you click the Constrain Proportions for Scaling button next to the scale fields in either palette, horizontal scale (Scale X) is automatically adjusted when you change vertical scale (Scale Y) and vice versa.

To manually resize a graphic but not its frame:

1. Choose the Direct Selection tool or the Position tool, and then click a graphic.

2. Drag any of the eight resizing handles. To maintain the graphic's proportions, hold down the Shift key when dragging.

## The Direct Selection Tool vs. the Position Tool

The Direct Selection tool and the Position tool are paired in the toolbox because they work similarly. Use the Position tool if you want to move a graphic within its frame or resize the frame. Use the Direct Selection tool if you want to move a graphic within its frame or change the shape of a frame by dragging an anchor point or segment.

## Live Display When Cropping and Scaling Graphics

If you pause briefly before man-ually resizing a graphics frame or moving a graphic within its frame, InDesign displays the graphic as you drag. Portions of the graphic that are outside the frame are ghosted (lightened) as you drag so that you can see exactly what's being cropped.

You can also change the scale of a selected graphic by modify-ing the Scale X Percentage or Scale Y Percentage values in the Con-trol palette or the Transform palette (**Figure 53b**). If the Constrain Proportions for Scaling button next to the scale fields in either pal-ette is enabled, horizontal scale (Scale X) is automatically adjusted when you change vertical scale (Scale Y) and vice versa.

Scale Y Percentage  Constrain Proportions When Scaling
Scale X Percentage

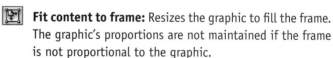

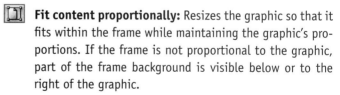

**Figure 53b** The Scale X Percentage and Scale Y Percentage fields in the Control palette show that the selected graphic is scaled to 50% of its original size. The Constrain Proportions When Scaling button to the right of the fields is selected, which means the graphic's proportions will be maintained if you change either of the scale values.

InDesign includes a set of fitting options that lets you resize a graphic to fit within its frame or resize a frame to fit the graphic. To use the fitting options, first select a graphic or a graphics frame. Next, click any of the five fitting buttons at the right end of the Control palette. The options are

**Fit content to frame:** Resizes the graphic to fill the frame. The graphic's proportions are not maintained if the frame is not proportional to the graphic.

**Fit content proportionally:** Resizes the graphic so that it fits within the frame while maintaining the graphic's pro-portions. If the frame is not proportional to the graphic, part of the frame background is visible below or to the right of the graphic.

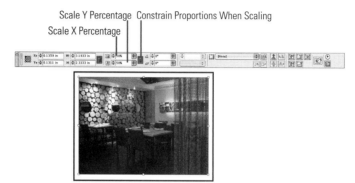

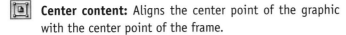 **Center content:** Aligns the center point of the graphic with the center point of the frame.

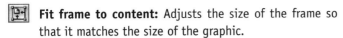 **Fit frame to content:** Adjusts the size of the frame so that it matches the size of the graphic.

**Fill frame proportionally:** Resizes the graphic so that it fills the frame while maintaining the graphic's proportions. If the frame is not proportional to the graphic, part of the graphic is cropped.

**Note**

*The Fitting buttons in the Control palette let you resize a graphic to fit its frame and vice versa. The same options are available in the Object menu (Object > Fitting).*

**The Info Palette**

When a graphic or frame that contains a graphic is selected, the Info palette (Window > Info) provides useful information about the graphic, including its file type (EPS, TIFF, Photoshop, etc.), actual and effective resolution (for pixel-based graphics), color space (RGB, CMYK, etc.), and ICC profile (if the graphic includes one).

# #54 Modifying Graphics and Graphics Frames

Cropping and scaling is only the beginning of what you can do to imported graphics with InDesign. You can also modify a graphic, its frame, or both by rotating, shearing (slanting), or flipping horizontally and/or vertically—not to mention applying any of several special effects that are explained in #55. In InDesign the controls for making basic modifications to graphics are available in the Control palette and the Transform palette (Window > Object & Layout > Transform).

As is the case with cropping and scaling, it's important that you make the correct selection before you modify a graphic. To modify a graphic and its frame, select the frame with the Selection tool. To modify only the graphic, select it with the Direct Selection or Position tool. If you look carefully, you'll notice that the border displayed around a selected graphics frame is a different color than the border that's displayed around a selected graphic.

Use the Control or Transform palette to make the following modifications (**Figure 54a**):

- **To change the selected object's position:** Change the X Location or Y Location value. If a graphics frame is selected, the values are measured from the ruler origin to the selected reference point, which is highlighted in the Reference Point button at the left of the Control and Transform palettes. If a graphic is selected, the values are measured from the reference point of the frame to the reference point of the graphic.

- **To make the selected object larger:** Change the Width or Height values. By default the accompanying Constrain Proportions for Width and Height button is selected, which means that changing either the Width or Height value will automatically change the other value to maintain the object's proportions.

- **To change the scale of the selection:** Change the values in the Scale X Percentage (horizontal scale) or Scale Y Percentage (vertical scale) fields. By default the accompanying Constrain Proportions When Scaling button is selected, which means that changing either the horizontal or vertical scale value will automatically change the other value to maintain the graphic's proportions.

- **To rotate the selection:** Enter a value other than 0 in the Rotation Angle field.

- **To shear the selection:** Enter a value other than 0 in the Shear X Angle field. Positive values slant the selection to the right; negative values slant it to the left.

The Control and Transform palette menus include additional commands for modifying objects, including Flip Horizontal, Flip Vertical, Flip Both, Rotate 180°, Rotate 90° CW, and Rotate 90° CCW.

**Other Ways to Modify Graphics**

In addition to the object modification controls in the Control and Transform palettes, similar functionality is available in the toolbox and the Object menu. Use any of the four transform tools—Rotate, Scale, Shear, and Free Transform—to modify a graphic by clicking and dragging. Double-click the Rotate, Scale, or Shear tool to display a dialog box that lets you specify various settings. Choosing Window > Object & Layout > Transform displays four options for modifying objects: Move, Scale, Rotate, and Shear. Choose any of these options to display a dialog box that lets you specify settings.

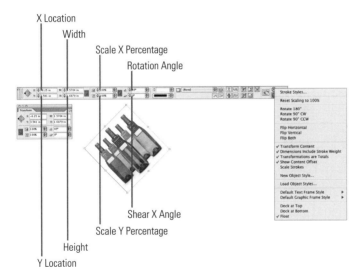

**Figure 54a** The Control and Transform palettes include controls for modifying graphics and graphics frames. In this example, the graphics frame—and the graphic within—are rotated 45°. Both palettes include menus with commands for modifying graphics and other objects.

**#54:** Modifying Graphics and Graphics Frames

## Modifying a Frame Without Affecting the Graphic

By default, Transform Content is checked in the Transform and Control palette menus for graphics frames. This means that when you modify a graphics frame, the modification is also applied to the graphic within. If you uncheck Transform Content for a graphics frame, transformations affect only the frame, not the graphic within.

You can also modify a graphics frame by adding a stroke (border) or a background fill or both. To add a stroke to a graphics frame:

1. Choose Window > Stroke to open the Stroke palette (**Figure 54b**).

2. Specify a stroke width in the Weight field and choose a stroke style from the Type menu in the Stroke palette. The Stroke palette includes other options that let you control the appearance of a stroke.

3. To specify the color of the stroke, click the Stroke icon in the toolbox or the Swatches palette, and then choose a color in the Swatches palette. If you want, you can apply a tint (shade) of the selected swatch by specifying a value in the Tint field at the top of the Swatches palette.

**Figure 54b** Use the Stroke palette to add a border around a graphics frame. In this example, the graphics frame has a 4-point double-striped stroke.

To add a background fill to a graphics frame, click the Fill icon in the toolbox or the Swatches palette, and then choose a color in the Swatches palette (**Figure 54c**). Optionally, specify a Tint value. A background fill is visible only outside the rectangle that contains the graphic—unless the graphic was saved with a transparent background or it's being displayed using a clipping path.

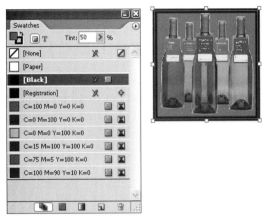

**Figure 54c** Use the Swatches palette to add a fill color to a graphics frame. In this example, the graphic is masked using a clipping path, and the graphics frame has a black background with a 50% tint.

## Applying Color to Grayscale and Black-and-White Graphics

If you want to modify the color of a graphic, you'll probably have to open the graphic file in its original application (for example, Photoshop or Illustrator). InDesign doesn't let you modify the color of an imported color graphic. You can, however, change the color of grayscale or one-bit (black and white) bitmap graphics. Select the graphic with the Direct Selection or Position tool, click the Fill icon in the toolbox or Swatches palette, and then click a swatch in the Swatches palette. Optionally, you can specify a Tint value in the Swatches palette.

# #55 Special Effects for Graphics

The Clipping Path command (Object menu) lets you mask portions of an imported graphic using built-in clipping paths or alpha channels or an InDesign-generated clipping path based on the graphic's contrast. While it's not possible to stroke a clipping path, you can convert a clipping path to a frame, and then apply a stroke to the frame. To change a clipping path into a frame:

1. Use the Clipping Path command to apply a clipping path.

2. Ctrl-click (Mac OS) or Right-click (Windows) and choose Convert Clipping Path to Frame from the context menu. After you convert a clipping path to a frame, you can apply a stroke to the frame, assign a frame style and color, and so on.

If you're looking for more exotic graphics modifications than simple rotation, scale, and shear, InDesign offers a handful of features that let you create see-through effects, or in InDesign terminology, "transparency effects." For example, you can make a graphic translucent so that underlying elements are visible through it. Or you can make the edge of a graphic fade to translucent and gradually reveal underlying elements.

Like the modifications explained in the previous two tips, you can apply transparency effects independently to a graphic and its frame. Make sure you use the correct tool to select the graphic or frame before you make your changes. Use the Selection tool to select the frame; use the Direct Selection or Position tool to select the graphic within. Generally, you'll apply these special effects to graphics frames; however, you can achieve different results by applying them to graphics—or both. Do whatever achieves the results you want.

InDesign includes four transparency effects:

- **Drop Shadow:** The Drop Shadow command (Object menu) lets you add a soft- or hard-edged shadow behind graphics and graphics frames (**Figure 55a**). The controls in the Drop Shadow dialog box let you specify the placement and appearance of the shadow. To create a hard-edged drop shadow, enter a Blur or Spread value of 0.

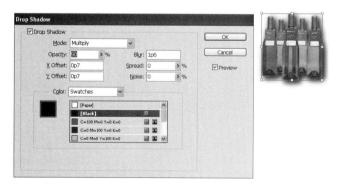

Figure 55a A drop shadow adds a three-dimensional look to a page. In this example, the drop shadow is applied to a graphic that has been silhouetted using a clipping path.

- **Feather:** The Feather command (Object menu) lets you fade the edge of a graphic or a graphics frame from opaque to transparent (**Figure 55b**). You can specify the distance over which feathering is applied. Underlying objects are visible through feathered areas.

Figure 55b The Feather dialog box lets you soften the edge of a graphic so that it fades to transparent. In this example, a feathered edge is applied to the graphic on the right.

- **Blending:** Like the blending mode feature in Photoshop, blending modes in InDesign provide options for blending the colors where objects overlap. Use the Blending Mode menu in the Transparency palette (Window >Transparency) to apply a blending mode to a graphic or graphics frame (**Figure 55c**).

Figure 55c The blending mode menu in the Transparency palette lets you apply any of several blending modes to a graphic. In this example, the Multiply blending mode is applied to the same graphic on the right.

(continued on next page)

---

**Applying Transparency to Other Objects**

You can apply InDesign's transparency effects to any object. For example, you can apply a drop shadow to text within a transparent text frame (a frame with no fill color), and you can apply a blending mode and opacity and feather the edges of shapes and lines you create with the drawing tools. When you apply a drop shadow to a transparent text frame, a drop shadow is created for all the text within the frame. You cannot apply a drop shadow to only a range of text.

## The Implications of Transparency

When you print or export an InDesign layout that includes transparency effects, such as drop shadows and feathered edges, InDesign *flattens* areas where transparency occurs. Flattening essentially rasterizes areas affected by transparent objects and sends this information to the printer for output. Although you're not likely to encounter any problems applying transparency effects or printing or exporting documents that contain transparency effects, it's a good idea to let your print service provider know if your documents contain transparency. Your service provider can make whatever adjustments are required to output the document correctly on its printers.

• **Opacity:** You can make a graphic or graphics frame appear to be translucent by applying opacity to it. Use the Opacity controls in the Transparency palette to modify the opacity of a graphic or graphics frame (**Figure 55d**). As you lower the opacity value, the selection becomes increasingly lighter and more translucent. An opacity value of 100% makes an object opaque. An opacity value of 0% makes an object invisible.

**Figure 55d** The Opacity field in the Transparency palette lets you make an object translucent. In this example, the graphic on the right has an opacity value of 50%, which reveals the shape beneath it.

If you want to mask portions of a graphic so that they're not visible, you can use a clipping path. The Clipping Path dialog box (Object > Clipping Path) lets you choose a clipping path or alpha channel that's built into a graphic, or you can choose Detect Edges in the Clipping Path dialog box's Type menu to have InDesign generate a clipping path based on the light and dark areas in the graphic (**Figure 55e**). The Detect Edges option works best for images that are silhouetted against a background that's uniformly lighter or darker.

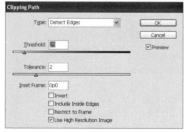

**Figure 55e** In this example, the Detect Edges option was used to create a clipping path for the graphic that removes the white background. The original graphic without a clipping path is on the left.

# #**56** Working with Illustrator Graphics

InDesign and Illustrator are close cousins and very much alike. They're both vector-based programs, they're both from Adobe, and they share many of the same features. One benefit of the similarity between Illustrator and InDesign is that you can copy objects between the two programs. This lets you take advantage of the features in both programs to create graphic elements.

The easiest way to add an Illustrator file to an InDesign layout is to use the Place command (File menu). When you place a graphic into a layout, InDesign maintains a link to the graphic file and uses the original file when displaying, printing, and exporting the graphic. (When you place an Illustrator graphic into an InDesign layout, you cannot modify any of the objects within the graphic. If you need to modify the graphic, you must open it in Illustrator and then make the changes.) Subsequent changes you make to the graphic file in Illustrator are reflected in the InDesign layout. Not only does InDesign support native Illustrator (.ai) files, it also supports illustrations saved as EPS or PDF.

In addition to importing Illustrator graphics into InDesign layouts, you can also copy and paste and drag and drop objects between the two programs. The benefit of being able to use these methods is that they let you use InDesign to modify objects you've created in Illustrator, and vice versa. Before you copy and paste or drag and drop Illustrator objects into InDesign, make sure to check AICB (Adobe Illustrator Clipboard) in the File Handling & Clipboard panel of Illustrator's Preferences dialog box (Illustrator > Preferences > File Handling & Clipboard [Mac OS]; Edit > Preferences > File Handling & Clipboard [Windows]).

To use the copy-and-paste method:

1. Select one or more objects in Illustrator.

2. Choose Edit > Copy.

3. Switch to InDesign and choose Edit > Paste. The copied elements are pasted into InDesign as a group of editable objects.

## Adjusting Layer Visibility in Illustrator Graphics

If you've created an Illustrator graphic that contains multiple layers and you want to place the graphic into an InDesign layout and then show or hide individual layers, you should save the graphic as a layered PDF file. When you save the PDF file (File > Save As), choose Acrobat 7 (1.6) or Acrobat 6 (1.5) in the Compatibility menu in the General panel of the Save Adobe PDF dialog box and check Create Acrobat Layers from Top-Level Layers.

When you import a layered PDF file into an InDesign layout, check Show Import Options in the Place dialog box. When you click OK, the Place PDF dialog box is displayed. Use the controls in the Layers panel to show and hide individual layers. After you've placed a layered PDF file, you can use the Object Layer Options command (Object menu) to adjust the visibility of the layers. (Note: In Illustrator, keep the layers that you want to show or hide in InDesign at the top level or within a layer set at the top level.)

To use the drag-and-drop method:

1. Arrange an Illustrator document window and an InDesign document window so you can see both onscreen.

2. Select one or more Illustrator objects, drag them into the InDesign window, and then release the mouse button.

When you copy and paste or drag and drop Illustrator objects into an InDesign layout, the objects behave as though you created them in InDesign, and InDesign does not maintain a link to the Illustrator file (that is, they're not listed in the Links palette).

Yet another option for working with Illustrator is to copy and paste or drag and drop InDesign objects into Illustrator, modify them in Illustrator, and then copy and paste or drag and drop the modified objects back into InDesign. This is called "round tripping." See **Figure 56** for an example.

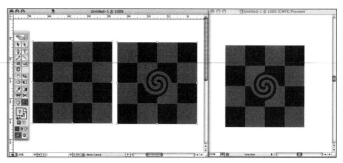

**Figure 56** The original checkerboard graphic (left) was created in InDesign, and then copied and pasted into an Illustrator document. Illustrator's Twirl tool was used to create the variation on the right, which was copied and pasted into the InDesign layout to complete the round trip.

# #57 Working with Photoshop Graphics

While the InDesign interface has more in common with Illustrator than Photoshop, InDesign and Photoshop are also tightly integrated. You can import native Photoshop (.psd) files into InDesign layouts, as well as other Photoshop-generated bitmap graphics, such as TIFF, JPEG, and DCS. InDesign's support of native Photoshop files also includes several features that let you control how images are displayed and printed.

## Show/Hide Layers and Layer Comps

When you import a Photoshop file that includes layers or layer comps, you can control the visibility of both within InDesign.

1. Choose File > Place.

2. Check Show Import Options in the Place dialog box, then click Open.

3. Display the Layers panel and make sure Show Preview is checked.

4. To achieve the result you want, do one of the following:

   - Choose a layer comp from the Layer Comp menu (**Figure 57a**).

   - Click the eye to the left of a layer name to alternately show or hide the layer

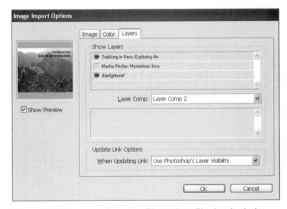

**Figure 57a** When you import a Photoshop file that includes layers or layer comps, you can use the controls in the Layers panel of the Image Import Options dialog to adjust the visibility of the layers and layer comps in the InDesign layout.

## Mask Portions of a Graphic

If you import a Photoshop file that contains clipping paths or alpha channels into an InDesign layout, you can use them to mask parts of a graphic or wrap text around them. To apply a clipping path or an alpha channel to a graphic:

1. Select the graphic or its frame, and then choose Object > Clipping Path.

2. In the Clipping Path dialog box, choose Alpha Channel or Clipping Path from the Type menu (**Figure 57b**). (If these options are not available, the graphic doesn't include any alpha channels or clipping paths.) If you choose Detect Edges in the Type menu, InDesign will generate a clipping path based on the light and dark areas of the image.

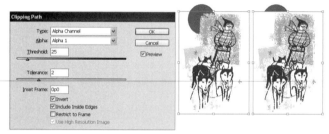

**Figure 57b** The original graphic, shown at the far right, has an opaque white background. Choosing an alpha channel and adjusting the settings in the Clipping Path dialog box produced the variation on the left. Notice how the circular shape is now visible through the background of the graphic.

## Display and Print Transparency

If you import a Photoshop file that includes transparency effects, such as a transparent background (instead of a clipping path) or a feathered edge, InDesign accurately displays and prints the effects.

# #58 Managing Graphic Links

Each time you place a graphic into an InDesign layout, InDesign collects and stores information about the graphic file, including its size, file type, link status (Up to Date, Modified, Missing, or Embedded), and location. InDesign uses the original graphic files when printing and exporting documents that contain imported graphics, as well as when displaying graphics at high resolution.

The Links palette (Window > Links) displays a list of all graphic files that have been placed in an InDesign layout and provides information about the files (**Figure 58**). It also includes commands and controls for managing the links between the document and the imported graphics.

Edit Original button
Update Link button
Go To Link button
Relink button

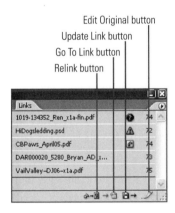

**Figure 58** The Links palette displays a list of all imported graphics and indicates the status of each one. In this example, the first graphic is listed as missing, the second is listed as modified, and the third is embedded in the document.

For each graphic file listed in the Links palette, InDesign displays the number of the page that contains the graphic and one of four status indicators:

- **Up to date:** If only the page number is displayed to the right of a graphic file, it means that the link is up to date (that is, the file is not missing and has not been modified since it was imported).

*(continued on next page)*

## Displaying Graphics at High Resolution

To display a selected graphic at high resolution, choose Object > Display Performance > High Quality Display. To enable high-resolution display for all imported graphics, open the Display Performance panel in InDesign's Preferences dialog box (InDesign > Preferences > Display Performance [Mac OS]; Edit > Preferences > Display Performance [Windows]), and then choose Default View > High Quality. InDesign uses the original graphic files to create high-resolution previews. If your graphic links aren't up to date, InDesign can't display them at high resolution. (Note: Displaying graphics at high resolution on older computers can noticeably slow down screen display.)

## Modifying Linked Graphics

As you work on a layout, you may need to modify an imported graphic. To quickly open an imported graphic in its original application, select the graphic or its frame, and then choose Edit > Edit Original. You can also select a graphic in the Links palette, and then choose Edit Original from the Links palette menu, or you can press Option (Mac OS) or Alt (Windows) and double-click a graphic.

**Missing:** The red missing link icon indicates that the graphic file has been moved or renamed since it was imported. To fix a missing link, click the Relink button at the bottom of the palette or choose Relink from the palette menu, and then locate and open the graphic file. If the graphic file has been modified since you imported it, the status indicator will change from Missing to Modified.

**Modified:** The yellow modified link icon indicates that the current version of the graphic file is more recent than the version used when the file was imported. To update the link, click the Update Link button at the bottom of the palette or choose Update Link from the palette menu.

**Embedded:** The embedded icon indicates that the graphic file has been embedded within the InDesign file. You can embed a graphic by selecting it in the Links palette, and then choosing Embed File from the Links palette menu. When you embed a graphic file, a copy of the file is stored within the InDesign file, and InDesign does not maintain a link to the original file. Any changes you make to the original file are not reflected in the InDesign document. Generally, it's not a good idea to embed graphic files within InDesign documents because InDesign file sizes can become prohibitively large.

If you want to see all of the information available for a particular graphic, double-click its name in the Links palette.

Although it's possible to display, export, and print documents that have modified or missing graphics, you should make sure all links are up to date before you perform any of these functions. If you try to export or print a document with missing or modified links, InDesign will warn you and let you update the links, or you can continue, in which case InDesign will use low-resolution graphics.

# CHAPTER SEVEN

# Working with Objects

No matter how comfortable you get with InDesign's drawing tools (see Chapter 5, "Drawing Lines and Shapes"), you'll want to modify nearly every object you create by applying a fill or a stroke, by scaling, rotating, or flipping horizontally or vertically, by moving or resizing, and so on. One of the most enjoyable benefits of using InDesign is that it allows you to change your mind as often as you want and modify objects in many ways. But before you can modify an object, you must first select it.

In this chapter you'll learn how to use two tools to select objects. The chapter also explains how you can use many of InDesign's most powerful features to modify objects and create eye-catching graphic elements.

# #59 Selecting and Deleting Objects

InDesign's toolbox has two tools for selecting objects: the Selection tool and the Direct Selection tool. Understanding the difference between these tools is critical if you want to work efficiently.

In most cases, you'll use the Selection tool ▶ to select objects. When you click an object with the Selection tool, the rectangular shape that encloses the object—its *bounding box*—is displayed with eight resizing handles around the perimeter and a center point in the middle. For rectangular objects, the bounding box and the shape of the object are identical. When you select a nonrectangular object with the Selection tool, you're actually selecting the bounding box rectangle that surrounds the object within (**Figure 59a**). You can drag a handle to resize a bounding box and the object within, and you can click within the object and drag to move it.

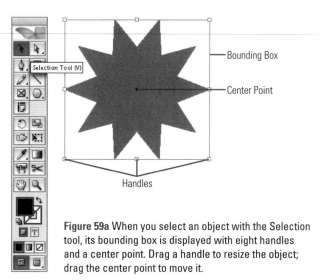

Figure 59a When you select an object with the Selection tool, its bounding box is displayed with eight handles and a center point. Drag a handle to resize the object; drag the center point to move it.

When you click an object with the Direct Selection tool ▶, the object's anchor points and segments are displayed, and you can drag them to change the object's shape (**Figure 59b**). You can also use the Direct Selection tool to click and drag a graphic within a graphics frame.

For rectangular objects—most text and graphics frames are rectangles—it's hard to tell the difference between an object and its bounding box. However, if you look closely at a rectangular frame selected with the Direct Selection tool, you'll see that anchor points are displayed only at the four corners, in contrast to the eight handles that are displayed if you use the Selection tool.

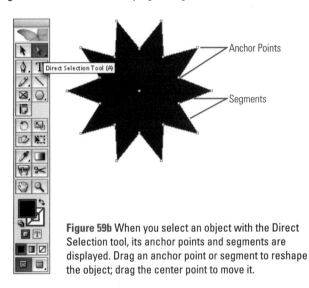

**Figure 59b** When you select an object with the Direct Selection tool, its anchor points and segments are displayed. Drag an anchor point or segment to reshape the object; drag the center point to move it.

Once you understand the difference between the Selection tool and the Direct Selection tool, you'll choose and use the right tool without a second thought. Here are a few more details you should know about selecting objects:

- Several commands for selecting objects and their contents are available in the Object menu. Choose Object > Select to display a list of commands for selecting objects above and below the currently selected object. If a graphic or graphics frame is selected, the Content and Container commands let you choose the graphic or its frame. If a group is selected, the Next Object in Group and Previous Object in Group commands let you select other objects in the group.

*(continued on next page)*

---

### Selecting an Empty Unassigned Frame

You can click anywhere within an empty graphics frame or text frame to select it, but if you click within an empty unassigned frame (for example, a frame created with the Rectangle, Ellipse, or Polygon tool), nothing happens. That is, the object is not selected. That's because you're actually clicking through the object and onto whatever is below, probably the page background. To select an empty unassigned frame, click its edge. You can then drag its center point to move it, resize its bounding box (if the Selection tool is selected), or reshape it by dragging anchor points and segments (if the Direct Selection tool is selected).

- You have two options for manually selecting multiple objects. Hold down the Shift key as you click objects with the Selection or Direct Selection tool, or click an empty area of the pasteboard or page and drag a rectangle that includes any portion of the objects you want to select.

- If the text insertion cursor is not flashing, choose Edit > Select All to select all objects on the page or spread.

- To temporarily switch to the Selection tool or Direct Selection tool when you're using another tool, press and hold the Command key (Mac OS) or the Control key (Windows). When you use this shortcut, InDesign switches to the tool (Selection or Direct Selection) that you most recently used.

- Use the Direct Selection tool to select an object that's part of a group. Click and drag the object's center point to move it; drag an anchor point or a segment to reshape the object. Switch to the Selection tool to select the object's bounding box.

The easiest way to delete an object is to select it with the Selection tool, and then press the Backspace or Delete key. You can also choose Edit > Clear. Choose Edit > Cut if you want to delete the object from its current location and paste it elsewhere (Edit > Paste). A cut or copied object is saved to the clipboard until you cut or copy something else or quit InDesign.

# #60 Moving and Locking Objects

One of the most common task's you'll perform when laying out pages is moving objects. This involves selecting text frames, graphics frames, and other graphic elements, and then repositioning them within a page or moving them to another page.

You have two options for moving objects:

- Use the Selection tool to manually move objects by clicking and dragging. If you hold down the Shift key when dragging an object, its movement is restricted to vertical, horizontal, and 45° angles.

- To move objects more precisely, change the X and Y values that specify an object's position relative to the zero point (the upper-left corner of the page by default). When an object is selected, the X Location and Y Location fields in the Control palette and Transform palette display the object's coordinates (**Figure 60**). By default, the X value represents the horizontal distance from the zero point to the object's center; the Y value represents the vertical distance from the zero point to the object's center. If you don't want to use an object's center point as the reference point, click one of the nine handles in the Reference Point icon at the left of the Control and Transform palettes.

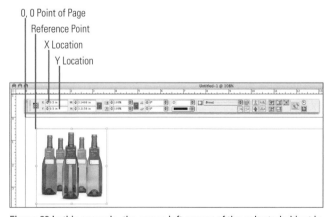

Figure 60 In this example, the upper-left corner of the selected object is its reference point. The X location and Y location values in the Control palette show that the upper-left corner of the object is one-half inch inside the left edge of the page and one-half inch below the top edge.

You can use the up/down, left/right arrow keys on your keyboard to nudge objects vertically and horizontally in small increments. By default, each click with an arrow key will move the selected object one point. To change the increment, open the Units & Increments panel of the Preferences dialog box and specify a different value for Cursor Key.

While it's possible to drag objects between adjacent pages, dragging objects to distant pages can get cumbersome. If you need to move an object to a different page, the Cut/Paste option is easiest.

1. Select the object.

2. Choose Edit > Cut.

3. Navigate to the page where you want to place the object, and then choose Edit > Paste. If you want to place the object in the same position on the new page as it was on the original page, choose Edit > Paste in Place.

If you want to prevent an object from being moved, select the object and then choose Object > Lock Position. When an object is locked, it can't be moved, either manually or by changing the X Location or Y Location value in the Control palette or Transform palette. You can, however, select and modify a locked object, for example, by applying a stroke or a background color. To unlock a locked object, select it, and then choose Object > Unlock Position.

# #61 Filling Objects with Color

If you use InDesign to create color publications, adding color to objects and changing the color of objects are common tasks. You can apply a background color—or in InDesign terminology, a *fill*—to any object. For example, you can apply color to a text frame to provide a nonwhite background for the text within it. You can apply color to objects you've created using InDesign's drawing tools. And in some cases, you can even apply a color to imported graphics.

You have two options for applying color to a selected object:

- The Swatches palette (Window > Swatches) lists a document's colors and gradients (**Figure 61a**). (See Chapter 8, "Working with Color" for information about creating colors and gradients.) Unless you have a good reason to use the Color palette, use the Swatches palette to apply color.

  Click the Fill box in the upper-left corner of the palette, and then click a color in the list. The Swatches palette also includes Tint controls that let you create color tints from 0% to 100%.

**Where's the Fill?**

If you choose a fill color only to discover—much to your surprise—that the selected object hasn't changed, make sure the Fill box—not the Stroke box—is selected in the Swatches palette, Color palette, or toolbox.

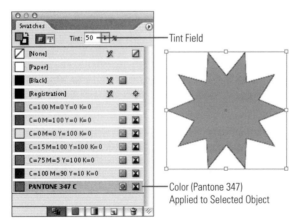

Tint Field

Color (Pantone 347) Applied to Selected Object

**Figure 61a** The Swatches palette lists a document's colors and lets you apply a color and a tint to selected objects. In this example, the object is filled with a 50% tint of Pantone 347.

*(continued on next page)*

## Applying Color to Pictures

You can apply color to imported black-and-white and grayscale images. Use the Direct Selection tool to select the image, and then click a color in the Swatches palette or create a color with the Color palette.

## Drag-and-Drop Color

In addition to the other ways mentioned to apply color, you can apply a fill or a stroke color to any object by dragging a swatch from a palette and dropping it onto the object or stroke you want to color.

- The Color palette (Window > Color; **Figure 61b**) lets you create colors on the fly—that is, without having to choose New Color Swatch from the Swatches palette menu. The downside is that these colors are not added to the document's color list, which means they don't show up in the Swatches palette, and you can't apply them to other objects unless you save or re-create them. (To save a color you've created with the Color palette, choose Add to Swatches from the palette menu or drag the swatch from the Color palette to the Swatches palette.)

Click the Fill box in the upper-left corner of the palette and choose a color model—RGB, CMYK, or Lab—from the palette menu. Use the controls to specify a color. The controls vary depending on the color model you select.

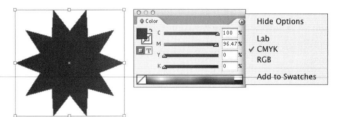

**Figure 61b** The Color palette provides controls for creating CMYK, RGB, and Lab colors.

In addition to the Fill boxes in the Swatches and Color palettes, there's a Fill box in the toolbox. Clicking any of these Fill boxes selects all three.

To remove an object's fill color, select the object and then click None or Paper in the Swatches palette. If you click None, the object is transparent. If you click Paper, the object is opaque white (unless you've modified the Paper swatch).

# #62 Adding a Stroke to Objects

Adding a stroke to an object can mean the difference between a mere graphic element and a graphic element that stands out on a page. For example, a stroke around a sidebar can set it apart from the surrounding elements and draw the reader's attention. Similarly, a stroke around a graphic can both contain the image within and isolate it from other elements.

The Stroke box is paired with the Fill box in the Swatches palette, Color palette, and toolbox, and the two work similarly. To add a stroke to a selected object, first click any Stroke box. (Note: By default, the Rectangle, Ellipse, and Polygon tools create objects with a one-point stroke.)

When you apply a stroke to an object, you may not be able to see it if it has no width or no color. The easiest way to specify a stroke's width is to choose a weight from the Weight menu in the Control palette or enter a weight value in the accompanying field (**Figure 62a**). The Stroke Type menu in the Control palette lets you choose a stroke style. (See the next how-to for information about adding custom stroke styles.)

Use the Swatches palette or the Color palette to assign a color to the stroke. (See the previous how-to for information about the Swatches and Color palettes.)

**Adding Corner Styles to Stroked Objects**

The Corner Effects command (Object menu) lets you apply any of five corner styles to stroked objects: Fancy, Bevel, Inset, Inverse Rounded, and Rounded. The Size field lets you control the size of the corner effect.

Stroke Type Menu
Stroke Weight Field

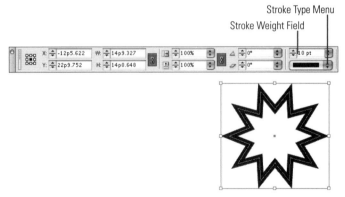

**Figure 62a** The Weight field in the Control palette specifies a 10-point-wide stroke. Below the Weight field, the Solid style is selected in the (Stroke) Type menu.

## Stroking Text

You can add a stroke to text and modify the appearance of the stroke the same as you do with objects. Highlight some text, click the Stroke box in the toolbox, Swatches palette, or Color palette, and then modify the stroke whichever way you want. When you add a stroke to highlighted text, the text remains editable.

## Switching an Object's Stroke and Fill

When applying fills and strokes to objects, it's easy to accidentally switch the stroke and fill colors. If you find yourself in this situation, click the Swap Fill and Stroke button in the Swatches palette, Color palette, or toolbox. This will switch the fill and stroke colors.

In addition to specifying a stroke's weight, type, and color, you can use the Stroke palette (Window > Stroke) to modify several other stroke characteristics (**Figure 62b**). The Stroke palette includes controls for specifying how segments connect and where the stroke is placed relative to the edge of the object (Align Stroke to Center, Align Stroke to Inside, or Align Stroke to Outside). You can also specify a Gap Color and Gap Tint for dashed, striped, and dotted stroke styles. The Start and End menus are available only for open paths and let you choose among several graphic endpoints, including arrowheads, squares, and circles.

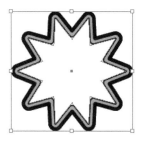

**Figure 62b** The Stroke palette includes several controls for modifying the appearance of a stroke. In this example, the stroke is 10 points wide and aligned with the outside of the object frame. A Thick-Thin (Stroke) Type is also applied, and the gap between the two strokes is 25% Black.

To remove a stroke from an object, select the object, and then set the stroke weight to 0. You can do this using the Weight field in the Control palette or the Stroke palette. You can also set the stroke color to None to remove a stroke from an object.

# #63 Creating Custom Stroke Styles

InDesign has 18 built-in stroke styles, ranging from stripes to dots, dashes, and hash marks. If these aren't enough for you, you can also create your own custom stroke styles.

To create a custom stroke style:

1. Choose Stroke Styles in the Stroke palette menu.

2. Click New in the Stroke Styles dialog box.

3. In the New Stroke dialog box (**Figure 63**), enter a name for the style and choose a Type: Stripe, Dotted, or Dash. Use the controls in the New Stroke Style dialog box to specify the appearance of the style, and then click OK to close the dialog box and save the style, or click Add to save the style and continue creating new styles.

**Sharing Stroke Styles**

Use the Save button in the Stroke Styles dialog box to share stroke styles with other InDesign users. When you save stroke styles, InDesign creates a separate file and assigns it a .Inst extension. Other InDesign users can click the Load button in the Stroke Styles palette, select a .Inst file, and click Open to add the stroke styles to a document. If no documents are open when you load stroke styles, they are added to the list of default styles and are automatically included in all new documents.

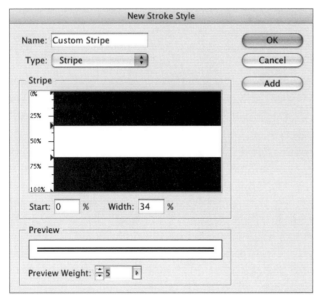

Figure 63 The controls for creating a custom stripe. The controls are slightly different for Dash and Dotted strokes.

There are too many controls in the New Stroke Style dialog box to attempt to explain each one. Fortunately, they're intuitive and easy to use. A few minutes of creative fiddling and you'll be comfortable.

After you create a new stroke style, it's displayed in the (Stroke) Type menu in the Control palette and the Stroke palette, and you can choose it when applying a stroke to an object or text.

If you want to modify the appearance of a custom stroke style, choose Stroke Styles in the Stroke palette menu, select the style in the list, and then click Edit. Make your changes, and then click OK to close the Edit Stroke Style dialog box. Click OK to close the Stroke Styles dialog box.

# #**64** Transforming Objects

InDesign provides many features that let you modify the appearance of an object. Four of these features are grouped together and referred to collectively as *transformations*:

- **Rotate:** Rotate objects from −180° to 180°.

- **Scale X Percentage:** Lengthen or shorten objects horizontally as a percentage of the current width.

- **Scale Y Percentage:** Lengthen or shorten objects vertically as a percentage of the current height.

- **Shear:** Specify a shear angle between −90° and 90° to slant an object along its horizontal axis.

As is true for many features, InDesign offers several methods for applying these transformations to selected objects:

- **Transform controls in the Control palette:** In addition to the four basic transformation controls—Rotate, Scale X Percentage, Scale Y Percentage, and Shear—the Control palette also includes controls for changing the location of an object (X and Y fields), as well as its Height and Width (H and W fields), for applying a stroke weight and style, and more (**Figure 64a**). The Control palette menu offers several additional commands for modifying objects, including Flip Horizontal, Flip Vertical, and Flip Both. It's the most versatile option for applying basic transformations and making other common changes to objects.

**Figure 64a** When an object is selected, the context-sensitive Control palette offers controls for modifying the position, size, and appearance of the object.

*(continued on next page)*

---

### Scaling Objects Manually

You can also scale objects manually using the Selection tool. Select an object with the Selection tool, and then click and drag a bounding box handle. Hold down the Shift key as you drag to maintain the object's proportion. To scale a graphics frame and the graphic within, hold down the Command key (Mac OS) or Control key (Windows) as you drag a bounding box handle. Add the Shift key to maintain the proportion of the graphic and the frame as you drag.

### Scaling Objects vs. Scaling Graphics

If you want to scale a graphic but not its frame, select the graphic with the Direct Selection tool, and then specify a Scale X Percentage or Scale Y Percentage value in the Control palette or the Transform palette, or drag one of the eight resizing handles on the graphic's border. Hold down the Shift key as you drag to maintain the graphic's proportions. If you need to know how much a graphic has been scaled, select it with the Direct Selection tool, and then check the Scale X Percentage and Scale Y Percentage values in the Control or Transform palette.

## Repeating Transformations

If you make one or more transformations to an object, InDesign remembers what you've done and lets you apply the transformations to other objects. To repeat transformations, select one or more objects, choose Object > Transform Again, and then choose one of the four options: 1) Transform Again applies the most recent change to the selected object. If multiple objects are selected, they're treated as a group. 2) Transform Again Individually applies the most recent change to each object separately if multiple objects are selected. 3) Transform Sequence Again applies the most recent succession of changes to the selected object. If multiple objects are selected, they're treated as a group. 4) Transform Sequence Again Individually applies the most recent succession of changes to each object separately if multiple objects are selected.

- **Transform palette:** The controls in the Transform palette (**Windows > Transform; Figure 64b**) are a subset of the controls in the Control palette, which is a good reason to use the Control palette unless you have a particular affinity for the Transform palette.

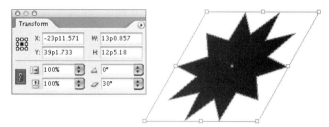

Figure 64b The Transform palette contains a subset of the controls available in the Control palette, including the four basic transformations: Rotate, Scale X Percentage, Scale Y Percentage, and Shear. In this example, a 30° shear angle is applied to the object.

- **Toolbox transformation tools:** The toolbox contains four transformation tools: Rotate tool, Scale tool, Shear tool, and Free Transform tool. There are two ways to use the Rotate tool, Scale tool, and Shear tool: 1) Select one of the tools, click an object to select it, and then click and drag; or 2) Select an object, and then double-click one of the tools. A dialog box is displayed with controls for specifying transformations. To use the Free Transform tool, select it, and then click an object. Drag a bounding box handle to scale the object. To rotate the object, move the pointer just outside a corner handle to display a rotation pointer ⤾, and then click and drag.

- **Transform commands:** The Transform commands in the Object menu provide yet another option for making basic transformations. Choose Object > Move, Scale, Rotate, or Shear to display a dialog box with controls for transforming the selected object.

If you want to maintain an object's proportions when scaling it horizontally or vertically, make sure the linked chain icon (not the broken chain icon) is displayed for the Constrain Proportions When Scaling button in the Control and Transform palettes. The Constrain Proportions When Scaling button has two states and two icons: 1) When the feature is enabled, the button shows as a linked chain. 2) When the feature is disabled, the button shows an unlinked chain. Clicking the button toggles between the two states.

# #65 Adding Drop Shadows

You can make an object appear to float above the surface of a page by applying a drop shadow to it. A drop shadow is placed beneath the selected object and makes it look like a light is casting the object's shadow onto the page and any underlying elements.

To create a drop shadow, select an object, and then choose Object > Drop Shadow. The controls in the Drop Shadow dialog box (**Figure 65a**) let you control the appearance and placement of a drop shadow. Here's a quick rundown of the controls:

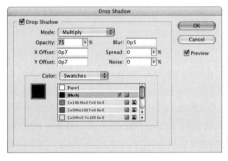

**Figure 65a** In this example, a drop shadow is applied to the clipping path of a placed graphic. You can also disregard the clipping path and apply the drop shadow to the frame.

- **The (Blending) Mode menu** lets you choose any of 16 blending modes. If a drop shadow overlaps any underlying objects, the selected blending mode determines how overlapping areas are displayed and printed.

- **The Opacity field** controls the shade and transparency of the shadow. Low Opacity values make the shadow lighter and more translucent. High Opacity values make the shadow darker and more opaque.

- **The X Offset and Y Offset fields** control the placement of the shadow. Negative values place the shadow above and to the left of the original. Positive values place the shadow below and to the right. If you set a drop shadow's X Offset and Y Offset values to 0, the shadow is placed directly beneath the object, creating a halo-like effect.

*(continued on next page)*

---

**Object Styles for Drop Shadows**

If you want to reuse drop shadow settings as you work on a layout, create an object style. First, create a drop shadow for an object using the settings you want to save. Second, select the object, and then choose New Object Style from the Object Styles palette (Window > Object Styles). Name the style and click OK to save it. After you create an object style, it's displayed in the Object Styles palette, and you can click it to apply it to a selected object. See #67 for more about Object Styles.

## Bring Text Frames with Drop Shadows to the Front

For best results when printing shadowed text that overlaps other objects, place the text frame at the top of the stacking order whenever possible. To move a frame to the top of the stacking order, select it, and then choose Object > Arrange > Bring to Front.

## Setting Drop Shadow Defaults for the Drawing Tools

If you open the Drop Shadow dialog box and specify drop shadow settings when no objects are selected, the settings are automatically applied each time you create a new object with the Rectangle, Ellipse, Polygon, Pen, and Pencil tools.

- **The Blur value** is the distance that's added to the selected object to create the shadow. Increasing the Blur value increases the size of the drop shadow. A blur value of 0 produces a hard-edged shadow that's the same size as the selected object.

- **The Spread value** controls the distance over which the shadow fades to transparent within the specified blur distance. Increasing the Spread value makes the shadow increasingly sharper. A Spread value of 100% creates a hard-edged drop shadow.

- **The Noise field** lets you add artifacts to a shadow to give it a grainier, courser appearance. Increasing the Noise value increases graininess.

- **The controls in the Color area** let you choose the color used for a drop shadow.

When you apply a drop shadow to a selected text frame, a shadow is created for all of the text within the frame (**Figure 65b**). You cannot create a drop shadow for highlighted text within a text frame. If a text frame has a fill color, the drop shadow is applied to the frame instead of the text. When you apply a drop shadow to a text frame, the text remains editable.

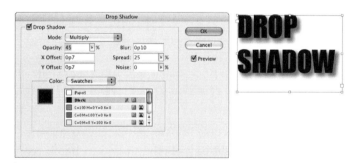

**Figure 65b** When you apply a drop shadow to a transparent text frame, all text within is included in the shadow.

To remove a drop shadow from an object, select the object, choose Object > Drop Shadow, and then uncheck Drop Shadow in the Drop Shadow dialog box.

# #66 More Special Effects for Objects

In addition to adding drop shadows to objects, you can apply one or more of three other special graphic effects: feathered edges, blending modes, and opacity. These three features, along with drop shadows, are collectively called *transparency effects* because they let you see through what would otherwise be opaque objects.

- **The Feather command** in the Object menu lets you soften the edge of an object so that the object fades from opaque to transparent approaching the edge (**Figure 66a**). The Feather Width value in the Feather dialog box controls the distance over which the object fades to transparent. The Corners menu offers three options for feathering corners: Diffused, Rounded, and Sharp. The Noise field lets you add artifacts to a feathered edge to give it a more grainy and course appearance. Increasing the Noise value increases graininess.

  If you apply feathering to a transparent text frame (that is, a text frame with a fill of None), the text within is feathered. If you apply feathering to a filled text frame, feathering is applied to the frame.

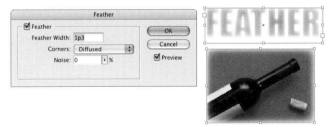

Figure 66a The Feather command lets you soften the edge of text and graphics. Underlying objects are visible in feathered areas.

*(continued on next page)*

## Printing and Exporting Transparency Effects

When you print pages that contain objects that are affected by transparency effects—drop shadows, feathered edges, blending modes, and opacity—or imported images (such as native Photoshop and Illustrator files) that contain transparency effects, areas affected by transparency are *flattened*. The flattening process converts areas where objects with transparency effects overlap into information that's sent to the printer. Flattening occurs in the background when you print and does not affect transparent objects on pages. Flattening can also occur when you export an InDesign file, for example, as an Acrobat 4 (PDF 1.3) file. If you send your InDesign layouts, or exported PDF versions of your InDesign layouts, to print service providers, it's a good idea to let them know if your files contain transparency effects.

- **The Blending Mode menu** in the Transparency palette (Window > Transparency) lets you apply any of 16 blending modes to an object (**Figure 66b**). The selected blending mode determines how colors are displayed and printed in areas where the object overlaps underlying objects. By default, the Normal blending mode is applied to objects. The Normal blending mode makes an object opaque unless its Opacity is less than 100%. (See the next bullet for more about Opacity.) The best way to get acquainted with the various blending modes is to try them on several objects. You can always switch back to Normal to prevent blending.

**Figure 66b** The two frames on the left have a black-to-white gradient fill. The Multiply blending mode is applied to the top frame. As the gradient gets lighter, the background graphic becomes more visible. The Normal blending mode is applied to the bottom frame, which makes it opaque.

- **The Opacity field** in the Transparency palette lets you make an object translucent (**Figure 66c**). An opacity value of 100% makes an object opaque. As you decrease the Opacity value, an object becomes increasingly lighter and translucent. An Opacity value of 0% makes an object transparent.

Figure 66c The two graphics on the top are in front of the background graphic. An opacity value of 50% is applied to the graphic on the top right, revealing the image below.

# #67 Using Object Styles

The ability to format text using character and paragraph styles is one of InDesign's most useful and powerful features. Object styles—a new feature in InDesign CS2—let you quickly format objects in much the same way character and paragraph styles let you format text. For example, if you create a newsletter that regularly uses sidebar text frames that include strokes, fills, and text insets, you can create an object style with these settings, and then use the object style to quickly format new sidebar frames.

Creating and using object styles is very much like creating and using character and paragraph styles, so if you're already familiar with character and paragraph styles, working with object styles is easy.

The easiest way to create an object style is to first modify an object manually so that it includes all the settings you want to include in the object style—fill color and tint, stroke weight and style, drop shadow, and so on. After the object is correctly formatted:

1. Open the Object Styles palette (Window > Object Styles) and choose New Object Style from the palette menu.

2. The New Object Style dialog box (**Figure 67a**) displays the settings applied to the selected object. Name the object style, and then click OK. The new object style is displayed in the Object Style palette.

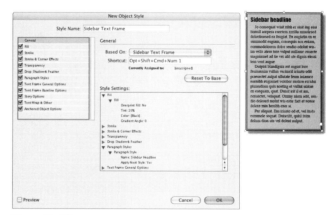

Figure 67a When you create a new object style, the settings applied to the selected object are used. In this example, the text frame has a tinted fill, a stroke, a drop shadow, and text insets.

You don't have to modify an object before you can create an object style. If you choose New Object Style from the Object Styles palette when nothing is selected, you can create the new object style from scratch by changing the settings in the New Object Style dialog box.

To apply an object style, select an object, and then click the name of the object style in the Object Style palette (**Figure 67b**) or use the keyboard shortcut, if you assigned one.

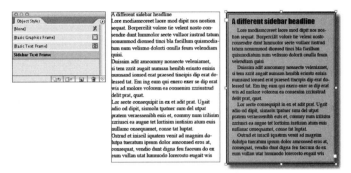

**Figure 67b** In this example, the Sidebar Text Frame object style was used to format the text frame on the right. The other text frame is the original, unstyled frame. Notice how the object style formatted both the frame and the text within. Because an object style can include a paragraph style, you can use object styles to format both text frames and the text within.

## Setting the Default Object Style for Frames

The Object Styles palette includes two default object styles: Basic Graphics Frame and Basic Text Frame. A small, square icon is displayed to the right of Basic Graphics Frame, indicating that this object style is used for new objects created with the Rectangle, Ellipse, and Polygon tools. A small, square icon with a T is displayed to the right of Basic Text Frame, indicating that this object style is used for new text frames created with the Type tool. You can drag either of these icons to other object styles to change the default style used for the Rectangle, Ellipse, Polygon, and Type tools.

# #68 Grouping Objects

There are times when you'll want to handle multiple objects as if they were a single object. For example, if you've placed a caption next to a photograph, you'll want to keep them together if you decide to move the photo. Or if you've created an illustration or a logo using several objects created with InDesign's drawing tools, you'll want to treat them as a single object when scaling, rotating, or shearing. The most efficient way to work with multiple objects at once is to create a group. In general, a group of objects behaves like a single object; however, you can still select and modify individual objects within a group.

To create a group, select two or more objects, and then choose Object > Group. (See #59 for more about selecting objects.) That's it.

To select a group, click any object with the Selection tool (**Figure 68**). A selected group is contained within a bounding box that has eight resizing handles and a center point. Click and drag any object to move the entire group. If you apply transformations, such as rotate, scale, shear, or flip horizontal/vertical, they're applied to the group as a whole rather than to each object individually.

**Figure 68** When you select a group, a rectangular bounding box with eight resizing handles is displayed around the perimeter of the grouped objects.

Selecting an object within a group can be a little tricky. You can't simply click it with the Selection tool because it selects the entire group. To select an object that's part of a group, click the object using the Direct Selection tool. If you want, you can then switch to the Selection tool, in which case the object behaves as though you selected it with the Selection tool in the first place.

If you click within a graphics frame using the Direct Selection tool, you select the graphic, not the frame. The easiest way to select a graphic frame within a group is to click the edge of the frame using the Direct Selection tool. If necessary, you can then switch to the Selection tool.

When an object that's part of a group is selected, the Select command (Object menu) displays two choices for selecting other objects within the group: Select Previous Object in Group and Select Next Object in Group. When a graphic or graphics frame is selected, you can choose Object > Select > Content and Object > Select > Container to select the graphic or the frame (whichever isn't selected).

To ungroup a group, select it, and then choose Object > Ungroup.

## Groups and Layers

When you create a group, all selected objects are stacked consecutively beneath the frontmost object. If you create a group from objects that are on different layers, all of the objects move to the layer of the frontmost object and are stacked consecutively beneath it.

## Nesting Objects

The Paste Into command (Edit menu) lets you place a copied object (that is, the last object you copied to the clipboard by choosing Edit > Copy or Edit > Cut) within a frame. The pasted object is said to be *nested* within the containing frame, which acts as a cropping shape for the pasted object. Selecting a nested object is like selecting an object in a group—click it with the Direct Selection tool.

# #69 Aligning Objects

You're probably already familiar with the concept of text alignment. InDesign provides several paragraph alignment options, including left-aligned, center-aligned, right-aligned, and justified. In much the same way as you control the alignment of lines in a paragraph, you can control the alignment of objects.

If you like icon-based user interfaces, you'll love the Align palette (Window > Object & Layout > Align). When two or more objects are selected, the 12 buttons in the Align palette let you control the placement of the objects relative to each other (**Figure 69**). Each button icon indicates graphically what will happen to the selected objects when you click the button.

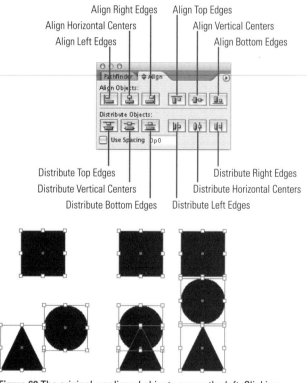

**Figure 69** The original, unaligned objects are on the left. Clicking Align Horizontal Centers in the Align palette produced the middle set. Clicking Distribute Vertical Centers produced the aligned and evenly spaced result on the right.

The six Align Objects buttons let you align objects along a vertical or horizontal axis. The six Distribute Objects buttons let you place a specified amount of space between objects along a horizontal or vertical axis. Each time you click a button, it's applied to the selected objects.

If you check Use Spacing in the Align palette, you can enter a value in the accompanying field that will be used to place space between the selected objects the next time you click one of the Distribute Objects buttons.

The six Align Objects buttons in the Align palette are also available in the Control palette when multiple objects are selected.

Getting the results you want using the Align palette takes a little practice. If you click one of the align/distribute buttons and don't like the results, you can always undo the action (Edit > Undo).

## Adding Space Between Objects

If you choose Show Options in the Align palette menu, the palette displays additional controls for specifying the vertical or horizontal space between selected objects. Check Use Spacing, and in the accompanying field, enter the amount of space you want to place between the selected objects. Then click the Distribute Vertical Space or Distribute Horizontal Space button.

# #70 Duplicating Objects

Sometimes in life, you have to do the same job more than once. Mowing your lawn and washing your clothes, for example. Fortunately, as an InDesign user, you never have to create the same object twice.

InDesign provides several options for making copies of objects. The one you choose depends on the number of copies you need and where you want to place them.

- **The Duplicate command** in the Edit menu creates a single copy of whatever's selected. The copy is placed 1 pica below and to the right of the original unless you've used the Step and Repeat command (see the last bullet item in this list), in which case the Horizontal Offset and Vertical Offset values used most recently in the Step and Repeat dialog box are used to place the duplicate.

- **Hold down Option (Mac OS) or Alt (Windows)** when you drag an object with the Selection tool or Direct Selection tool to create a duplicate of the object (**Figure 70a**). The copied object is placed where you release the mouse button. The original object is unchanged. If you hold down the Shift key when you Alt/Option+drag an object, you can drag only in increments of 45°.

**Figure 70a** If you hold down the Option key (Mac OS) or the Alt key (Windows) when dragging an object with the Selection tool or Direct Selection tool, a pair of arrow pointers is displayed as you drag. The white one indicates that you're dragging a copy of the original object. If you pause briefly before Alt/Option+dragging an object, the duplicate is displayed as you drag.

- **The Copy and Paste commands** in the Edit menu provide another option for duplicating an object. Whatever you copy with the Copy command is saved to the clipboard until you copy or cut something else. The Edit menu also provides three choices for pasting copied objects: 1) choose Paste to place copied objects in the middle of the currently displayed page; 2) choose Paste Into to place the copied object into a selected frame and create a nested object; or 3) choose Paste in Place to place the selected objects using the X and Y offsets of the original objects. This is a handy option if you want to copy something onto a new page while retaining the position of the original.

- **The Step and Repeat command** in the Edit menu lets you create multiple copies of an object and specify the placement of the copies relative to the original (**Figure 70b**).

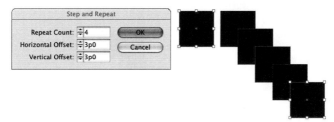

**Figure 70b** The Step and Repeat command (Edit menu) lets you create multiple duplicates in a single operation. In this example, the settings in the Step and Repeat dialog box produced the final result at the right from a single frame.

## Store Objects in Libraries and as Snippets

If you want to save a copy of an object for use in other documents, you can save the object in an InDesign library or you can create a *snippet* file. You can share both libraries and snippet files with colleagues and clients. See #72 for more about libraries; see #73 for more about snippets.

# #71 Changing the Stacking Order

## Moving an Object to a Different Layer

You can use the Layers palette to move an object to a different layer. Select the object, and then open the Layers palette. Drag the small, colored square that's displayed to the right of the name of the highlighted layer to another layer. The object is placed at the top of the stacking order on its new layer. Then use the Arrange options to change the object's placement within the layer's stacking order.

Every object on a page occupies a specific place in the page's *stacking order*. The first object you create on a page is placed at the bottom of the stack of objects. Each new object is placed successively higher in the stack.

If objects don't overlap, their stacking order is not important; however, if objects overlap, the stacking order determines which object is visible in the overlapping areas. You may find that you need to move objects forward or backward in the stacking order to create the desired result (**Figure 71**).

The Arrange command (Object menu) displays four options for changing the position of the selected object in the stacking order:

- **Bring to Front:** Moves an object to the top of the stack.

- **Bring Forward:** Moves an object one level higher in the stack.

- **Send Backward:** Moves an object one level lower in the stack.

- **Send to Back:** Moves an object to the bottom of the stack.

Figure 71 Four objects are stacked upon each other (left). The text frame is at the top of the stack; the empty circular frame is at the bottom. Selecting the circular frame and choosing Object > Arrange > Bring to Front produced the result on the right.

Layers have their own stacking order the same as objects. (For more about layers, see #82.) When you choose any of the four Arrange commands (Bring to Front, Bring Forward, Send to Back, and Send Backward), the selected object moves forward or backward only within its own layer. This means, for example, that if you choose Object > Arrange > Bring to Front, the selected object may not be the frontmost object if it's on a layer that's below another layer. To place an object in front of all other objects, move it to the front of the frontmost layer.

If you place objects on a master page, they're placed at the bottom of the stacking order behind objects that you place on the same layer on a document page. If you want to place master objects in front of objects on document pages, create a layer for the master objects and place that layer on top of the layer you use for objects on document pages.

### Selecting an Object That's Behind Another Object

If you need to select an object that's behind another object, one option is to select the frontmost object, and then move it backward so that you can see and then select the object that was behind it. If you hold down the Command key (Mac OS) or the Control key (Windows) and click an area where multiple objects overlap, each click selects the next lowest object in the stacking order. Once you reach the bottom object, the next Command/Control-click selects the topmost object.

# #72 Using Libraries

InDesign libraries provide quick access to objects you use repeatedly—such as logos, boilerplate text, house ads, frequently used graphics, and so on. A library file is essentially a collection of objects, and an open library file is displayed as a palette with thumbnail previews of the objects it contains. It's easy to place objects into libraries, and it's just as easy to place copies of library objects onto pages.

Using libraries requires three steps:

1. **Create a library.** To do this, choose File > New > Library. Name and save the library. Library files are automatically assigned a .indl extension to differentiate them from InDesign layouts, which are assigned a .indd extension. After you click Save, an empty library window is displayed with the name you assigned in the tab. You can create as many different library files as you want. For example, you might have one library named "Frequently Used Corporate Logos" that contains nothing but logos and another named "Disclaimer Text" that contains nothing but text frames with different kinds of legal copy.

2. **Add objects to the library.** Select one or more objects, and then drag them into the library palette (**Figure 72a**). Generally, you'll want to add objects that you're likely to use repeatedly. You can add any object or multiple-selected objects to an open library, and there's virtually no limit to the number of objects a library can contain.

**Figure 72a** A library palette displays thumbnails of the objects it contains. Click and drag a thumbnail onto a page or the pasteboard to add a library object to a document.

**3. Place library objects into documents.** Click and drag a thumbnail from the library palette onto a page or the pasteboard. You can navigate to a different page, open a new document, or switch to a different document window if multiple documents are open. In each case, simply drag a thumbnail from the library palette to the document window to add the object to the document.

Double-click a thumbnail in a library palette to display the Item Information dialog box, which lets you assign a name to the object, add a comment, and assign any of seven object types (**Figure 72b**). You can sort and search for library objects based on their name and other information.

### Sharing Libraries

Although it's possible to share libraries that are stored on a server or a shared computer, only one InDesign user at a time can open a library file unless the file is locked. If you lock a library file, multiple users can open it simultaneously, but none of them can add objects to or delete objects from the library.

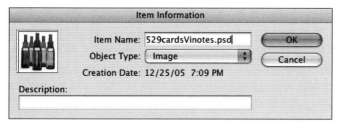

**Figure 72b** You can assign a name to a library object, add a description, and choose an object type, and you can use this information to sort and locate objects within a library.

The library palette menu includes several other useful commands for working with libraries:

- **Add Item:** Adds the selected object to the library.

- **Add Items on Page:** Adds all objects on the currently displayed page to the library as a single object.

- **Add Items on Page as Separate Objects:** Adds all objects on the currently displayed page to the library as separate objects.

*(continued on next page)*

- **Update Library Item:** If you drag a thumbnail from a library palette to a document, and then change the object in the document, click Update Library Item to apply the changes you made to the library object.

- **Place Item(s):** Places the objects selected in the library palette into the active document.

- **Delete Item(s):** Removes the objects selected in the library palette from the library.

- **Sort Items:** Lets you sort library objects based on Name, Oldest, Newest, and Type.

It's worth noting that if you add a graphics frame containing a graphic to a library, InDesign does not save the original graphic file in the library file—it saves only the path to the original file and a low-resolution preview. If you intend to share the library, you'll also have to provide the graphics file for users of the library to display and print the graphic at the highest possible resolution.

To close a library window, click the close button in the upper-left corner. Library palettes behave like other palettes, which means you can dock them to the edge of your monitor, expand and collapse them, group them with other palettes, and so on. Choose File > Open to open an existing library.

# #73 Using Snippets

Snippets are similar to libraries in that you can use them to save and share InDesign objects. A snippet is an electronic file that contains one or more InDesign objects. Snippet files are much like graphic files—for example, you can import or drag and drop them into InDesign layouts; however, you create snippets with InDesign rather than a graphic program, such as Photoshop or Illustrator. A snippet stores not only InDesign objects—text frames, graphic frames, lines, and so on—but their page location and other information as well. This means that when you place a snippet into a layout, the objects retain their original appearance and their original position.

Like a library, you must create a snippet before you can use it in other InDesign documents or share it with other InDesign users. To begin, select one or more objects that you want to save and reuse. You can then use any of three methods to create a snippet:

- Choose File > Export to display the Export dialog box, and then choose InDesign Snippet from the Format menu. Name the file and choose a storage folder. Snippet files are automatically assigned a .inds extension.

- Drag the selected objects into the Bridge window and drop them onto a volume or folder icon or into the open volume or folder (**Figure 73**). The snippet file is automatically given a name that begins with "Snippet." You can change the name of the file, but you should keep the .inds filename extension.

*(continued on next page)*

## Graphics in Snippets

If you create a snippet that includes a graphics frame that contains an imported graphic, only the path to the graphic file is saved in the snippet. If you want to share the snippet, you should include a copy of the graphic file along with the snippet file or provide users with the path to the graphic file.

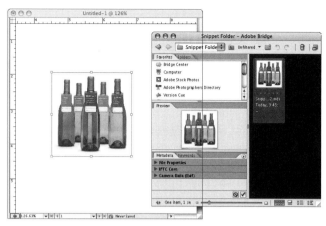

**Figure 73** The graphics frame in the InDesign document window on the left was dragged into the Bridge window on the right to create a snippet.

- Drag and drop the selected objects onto the desktop or onto a volume or folder icon on the desktop. The snippet file is given a name beginning with "Snippet." You can change the name of the file but keep the .inds extension.

After you create a snippet, you can use it repeatedly in your InDesign layouts or provide it to other InDesign users who can use it in their layouts. You have two options for placing a snippet into a layout:

- Use the Place command (File menu) to import a snippet in the same way as you import a graphic.

- Drag a snippet file from the Bridge window, the Mac OS Finder, or Windows Explorer and drop it into an InDesign document window.

# CHAPTER EIGHT

# Working with Color

Adding color to a publication can make the difference between drab and dazzling. InDesign provides many features for creating several different kinds of colors and applying them to text and objects.

In this chapter you'll learn how to use commands in the Swatches palette to add process and spot colors, tints, multicolor gradients, and mixed ink colors to a document and how to use the Gradient and Color palettes to quickly build and apply gradients and colors on the fly. In addition, we'll take a brief look at InDesign's color management capabilities and show you how to specify color settings.

# #74 Using Spot Colors, Process Colors, and Tints

The best way to use spot and process colors is to begin by adding them to a document, after which you can apply them to text, fills, and strokes. The Swatches palette (Windows > Swatches) displays a list of available colors, including spot colors, process colors (CMYK), tints, gradients, and mixed ink colors, as well as controls for creating new colors and working with colors.

Adding a spot color or a process color is much the same. To add a spot color:

1. Choose New Color Swatch from the Swatches palette menu.

2. In the New Color Swatch dialog box (**Figure 74a**), choose Spot in the Color Type menu, and then choose a spot color library in the Color Mode menu.

3. Select a color from the scroll list or enter a number in the field above the scroll list.

4. Click OK to add the color to the Swatches palette and close the dialog box, or click Add to add the color to the Swatches palette and keep the dialog box open so you can add more swatches.

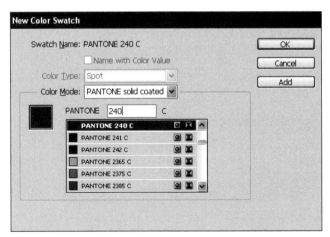

**Figure 74a** In this example, a Pantone Solid Matte spot color—Pantone 240—is defined in the New Color Swatch dialog box.

To add a process color:

1. Choose New Color Swatch from the Swatches palette.

2. In the New Color Swatch dialog box (**Figure 74b**), choose Process in the Color Type menu, and then choose CMYK or a process color library, such as FOCOLTONE or TRUMATCH in the Color Mode menu. If you choose CMYK, use the Cyan, Magenta, Yellow, and Black controls to define the color. If you check Name with Color Value, a process CMYK color is automatically assigned a name that includes its CMYK percentages (for example, C=30 M=100 Y=50 K=0). If you don't check Name with Color Value, you can assign your own name.

3. Click OK to add the color to the Swatches palette and close the dialog box, or click Add to add the color to the Swatches palette and keep the dialog box open so you can add more swatches.

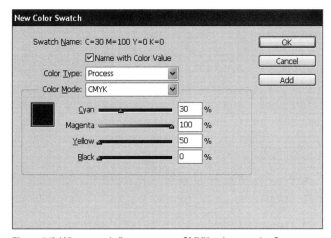

**Figure 74b** When you define a process CMYK color, use the Cyan, Magenta, Yellow, and Black controls to specify the percentage of each process color.

**Adding Default Colors to the Swatches Palette**

If you create new color swatches—spot color, process color, tint, gradient, or mixed ink—when no documents are open, they are saved as program-level defaults and are automatically included in all new documents. If you create new colors when a document is open, the colors are specific to that document.

## Using the Eyedropper Tool to Add Colors from Graphics

You can use the Eyedropper tool to "pick up" colors from imported graphics, and you can save these colors and apply them to other objects. To add a color from an imported graphic to the Swatches palette list, select the Eyedropper tool, and then click within an imported graphic. The pixel you click on is used, so you might want to zoom in before you click. After you click, the color of the pixel you clicked on is displayed in the Fill box in the toolbox, the Swatches palette, and the Color palette. Drag any of these fill boxes to the Swatches palette list to add the color to the document. Clicking an RGB image creates an RGB color; clicking a CMYK image creates a CMYK color.

After you create a color, it is added to the list of swatches in the Swatches palette, and you can apply it to text, fills, and strokes. (See #61 Filling Objects with Color and #62 Adding a Stroke to Objects for information about applying color to fills and strokes.) The spot color icon ▣ is displayed to the right of the names of spot colors in the Swatches palette; the process color icon ▦ is displayed to the right of the process colors.

If an object is selected when you create a new color, the color is applied to the object's stroke or fill, depending on whether the Stroke box or the Fill box is selected in the toolbox. If nothing is selected when you create a new color, the color becomes the default fill color or stroke color for new objects (except objects created with the three frame tools), depending on whether the Stroke box or Fill box is selected in the toolbox.

If you want to apply a tint of a color to an object instead of applying the color at full intensity, use the Swatches palette to first apply the color, and then use the Tint controls in the Swatches palette to assign a tint value between 0% and 100%. The lower the Tint value, the lighter the color.

You can also add tints to the list of swatches in the Swatches palette, and then apply them to objects in the same way as you apply other swatches. To add a tint of a color, select the color in the Swatches palette list, and then choose New Tint Swatch from the palette menu. Use the Tint controls in the New Tint Swatch dialog box to specify a tint value.

The Swatches palette and its menu (**Figure 74c**) contain many controls and commands for working with colors. In addition to commands for creating new spot and process colors, tints, gradients, and mixed ink colors, the Swatches palette menu includes commands for:

- Deleting (Delete Swatch) and modifying swatches (Swatch Options)

- Exporting (Save Swatches for Exchange) and importing (Load Swatches) swatches

- Displaying swatches in the palette (Name, Small Name, Small Swatch, Large Swatch)

**Figure 74c** The Swatches palette displays a list of available colors and includes many controls and commands for creating and managing colors.

**#74**: Using Spot Colors, Process Colors, and Tints

# #75 Using Gradients

A gradient is a smooth transition from one color or tint to another color or tint. A well designed and well placed gradient adds movement and contrast to a page—both of which add visual appeal. InDesign lets you create multicolor gradients and apply them as fills and strokes to text and objects.

## Creating Gradients Using the Swatches Palette

The most efficient way to use a gradient is to first add it to the Swatches palette list, after which you can apply it to text and objects.

To create a gradient:

**1.** Open the Swatches palette (Window > Swatches) and choose New Gradient Swatch from the Swatches palette menu.

**2.** In the New Gradient Swatch dialog box (**Figure 75a**), enter a name for the gradient in the Swatch Name field and choose Linear or Radial from the Type menu.

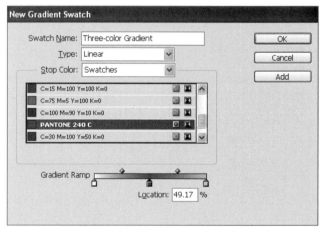

**Figure 75a** The controls in the New Gradient Swatch dialog box let you choose a gradient's colors.

**3.** The Gradient Ramp displays the gradient. Below the ramp, color stops—the small, colored squares—show the colors in the gradient. Above the ramp, small diamonds indicate the midpoints between pairs of colors. To specify the start color, click the white square at the left end of the Gradient

Ramp, and then use the controls in the Stop Color area to assign a color. Click the black square at the right end of the Gradient Ramp to specify the end color. The controls in the Stop Color area vary, depending on the choice you make in the Stop Color menu. If you choose Lab, CMYK, or RGB, the controls let you create new colors. If you choose Swatches, the document's swatches (spot and process colors, gradients, tints, and mixed ink colors) are listed.

4. To add a color to a gradient, click just below the ramp. A color stop is added where you click. Use the controls in the Stop color area to change the color.

5. To delete a color from a gradient, click its color stop and drag downward. You can also modify a gradient by dragging color stops and midpoints or by selecting a color stop or midpoint and changing the Location value.

6. When you're ready to save a gradient, click OK to add the gradient to the Swatches palette and close the dialog box, or click Add to add the gradient to the Swatches palette and keep the dialog box open so you can add more gradients. After you create a gradient, you can apply it to text and objects, and fills and strokes in the same way you apply spot and process colors (**Figure 75b**).

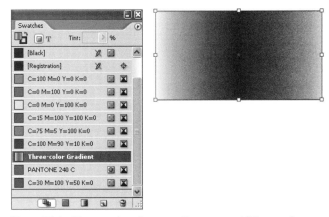

Figure 75b In this example, a linear gradient—named "Three-color Gradient"—is used to fill an empty frame.

**#75: Using Gradients**

## Creating See-through Gradients

Although you can't use None (transparent) as a color in a gradient, it is possible to create a gradient that goes from opaque to transparent. Create a gradient that includes white (Paper color), for example, a simple black-to-white gradient. Fill a frame with the gradient, and then apply the Multiply blending mode to the frame (Window > Transparency; Blending Mode menu > Multiply). Place the frame in front of another object. White areas in the gradient are transparent, and as the blend gets darker, it becomes less transparent.

## Creating Gradients Using the Gradient Palette

In addition to creating gradient swatches that are displayed in the Swatches palette list, you can use the Gradient palette (Window > Gradient) to create gradients on the fly. If you create a gradient using the Gradient palette, the gradient is applied to the fill or stroke of selected text or objects, depending on whether the Fill box or the Stroke box is selected in the toolbox. If nothing is selected when you create a gradient, it becomes the default stroke or fill for new objects created with the drawing tools (with the exception of the three frame tools).

The controls in the Gradient palette are similar to the controls in the New Gradient Swatch dialog box, though not identical. The gradient ramp works the same as the gradient ramp in the New Gradient Swatch dialog box with one exception: To add a color stop, drag a swatch from the Swatches palette and release it on the ramp. Release the swatch on an existing color stop to replace it. The Type menu and Location fields are the same as those in the New Gradient Swatch dialog box. The Reverse button lets you flip a gradient, and the Angle field lets you rotate a linear gradient.

Gradients you create with the Gradient palette are not automatically added to the Swatches palette list. If you want to save a gradient you create with the Gradient palette, drag the Fill box from the Gradient palette to the Swatches palette.

## Using the Gradient Tool

The Gradient tool provides another option for applying a blend. To use the Gradient tool, first apply a gradient to the fill or stroke of an object or text. With the object or text still selected, select the Gradient tool, and then click and drag on the page. The spot where you click is the start point of the blend; the spot where you release the mouse is the endpoint of the blend (**Figure 75c**).

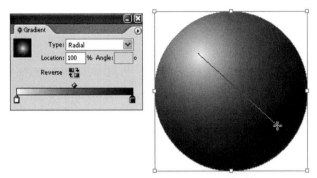

**Figure 75c** In this example, clicking and dragging with the Gradient tool produces a slightly off-center radial blend. The white/highlight spot is the start point; the crosshair pointer indicates the endpoint.

# #76 Using Mixed Ink Colors

In addition to creating and applying spot and process colors, tints, and gradients, you can create mixed ink colors that combine a spot color with one or more spot or process colors. For example, if you're working on a publication that uses black and one Pantone color, you can create a mixed ink color that combines a tint of black and the Pantone color.

To create a mixed ink color:

1. Open the Swatches palette (Window > Swatches) and choose New Mixed Ink Swatch from the Swatches palette menu.

2. In the New Mixed Ink Swatch dialog box (**Figure 76a**), enter a name for the mixed ink. (It's a good idea to include the names and percentages of the component colors.)

3. Click the empty square to the left of each color you want to include.

4. For each color you choose, enter a tint value from 0% to 100% by adjusting the slider or entering a value in the % field.

5. When you're done choosing colors and specifying tints, click OK to add the mixed ink color to the Swatches palette and close the dialog box, or click Add to add the mixed ink color to the Swatches palette and keep the dialog box open so you can add more mixed ink colors. After you create a mixed ink color, you can apply it to text and objects, and fills and strokes in the same way as you apply spot and process colors.

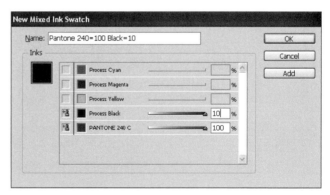

**Figure 76a** The New Mixed Ink Swatch dialog box lets you create a swatch that combines tints of one or more colors. In this example, a spot color—Pantone 240— is mixed with a 10% tint of black.

You can create mixed ink color swatches one at a time by choosing New Mixed Ink Swatch from the Swatches palette menu, or you can choose New Mixed Ink Group to create several variations of a particular combination of colors at once. In the New Mixed Ink Group dialog box (**Figure 76b**), select the colors you want to include by clicking the empty box next to them. For each color specify:

- The percentage of the starting tint in the Initial field.

- The number of times you want to repeat the increment in the Repeat field.

- The amount of change between tints in the Increment field.

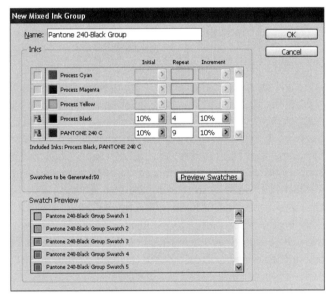

**Figure 76b** The New Mixed Ink Group dialog box lets you mix several combinations of tints and colors at once. In this example, a Pantone spot color—Pantone 240—is combined with black. Then, 10% tint increments of Pantone 240 (starting at 10% and repeating 9 times) are mixed with 10% tint increments of black (starting at 10% and repeating 4 times). These settings produce a group with 50 mixed ink colors. You can see the first five colors in the Swatch Preview area.

### Can't Create a Mixed Ink Color?

The Create New Mixed Ink command is available in the Swatches palette menu only if the Swatches palette list includes at least one spot color. A mixed ink color must have at least one spot color.

# #77 Using the Color Palette

Like the Gradient palette, you can use the Color palette (Window > Color) to create colors on the fly—that is, without having to open the New Color Swatch dialog box. Generally, it's a good idea to choose New Color Swatch from the Swatches palette menu when you need a new color because the color is added to the Swatches palette list and you can apply it whenever you want. That said, the Color palette (**Figure 77**) provides a quick alternative for creating colors.

The controls in the Color palette are similar to the controls in the New Color Swatch dialog box. To create a color:

1. Choose Lab, CMYK, or RGB from the palette menu to specify the kind of color you want to create. The color controls displayed depend on the selected color model. A color spectrum is displayed below the tint percentage fields and sliders.

2. Click the spectrum or use the fields and sliders to specify color settings.

To add the color in the Color palette to the Swatches palette list, choose Add to Swatches from the Color palette menu, drag the Fill box from the Color palette to the Swatches palette, or click the New Swatch button at the bottom of the Swatches palette. To add all colors you've applied using the Color palette to the Swatches palette, choose Add Unnamed Colors from the Swatches palette menu.

When you create a color using the Color palette, it's applied to the current selection. If nothing is selected, the color is the default color for the fill or stroke of new objects (except for frames created with any of the three frame tools), depending on whether the Fill box or the Stroke box is selected in the Color palette or toolbox.

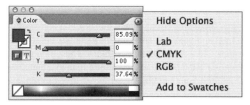

Figure 77 Use the Color palette to quickly create new colors without having to open the New Color Swatch dialog box.

# #78 Setting Up Color Management

A brief how-to about color management is a little like providing a brief how-to about nuclear physics. Thick books by smart people have been written about the physics, physiology, and psychology of color and managing color in a publishing workflow. It's hard to reduce the topic of color management to a single bit of advice. That said, it's easy to enable InDesign's color management feature, and with minimal effort, you can set up a simple color-managed workflow so that colors look as consistent as possible throughout your workflow and under various display and print conditions.

By default, color management is turned on in InDesign. If you use InDesign as part of Adobe Creative Suite, you can use Adobe Bridge to synchronize color settings across all applications so that colors look the same throughout the suite.

To set up color management in InDesign, choose Edit > Color Settings. The Settings menu in the Color Settings dialog box (**Figure 78**) offers four options. Choose the option that is most appropriate for the kinds of publications you create with InDesign:

- Choose Monitor Color only if you create designs for video or onscreen presentation.

- Choose North America General Purpose to use typical settings for publications that will be printed with desktop printers (laser and inkjet) and for onscreen publications in North America.

- Choose North America Prepress to use typical settings for publications that will be printed on a printing press in North America.

- Choose North America Web/Internet to use typical settings for onscreen presentation in North America.

## Synchronizing Color Settings Across Adobe Creative Suite

Although it's possible to specify custom color settings for each application in Adobe Creative Suite, it's usually a good idea to synchronize color settings across all applications. To do this, open Adobe Bridge and navigate to the Bridge Center. If color settings are not synchronized, the color settings button at the bottom of the Bridge window displays, "Color Management is not synchronized." Click the button to display the Suite Color Settings dialog box. Click a setting in the list, and then click Apply.

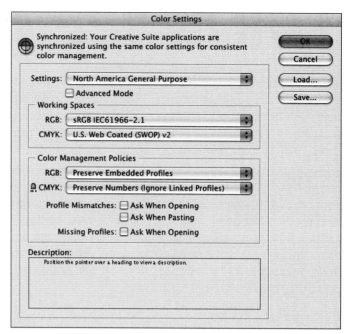

**Figure 78** One option for managing color in InDesign is to choose one of the built-in settings available in the Settings menu.

If you're knowledgeable about color management and aren't satisfied with the default settings in the Color Settings dialog box, you can specify custom settings. Click Save to save custom settings in a file you can share with colleagues and clients.

If you use InDesign as part of Adobe Creative Suite, InDesign's color management settings are automatically synchronized with the other applications. When you first open the Color Settings dialog box, Synchronized is displayed in the upper-left corner to let you know that the settings are in synch with the other Creative Suite applications. If you change any of the settings in the Color Settings dialog box, Synchronized changes to Unsynchronized.

# CHAPTER NINE

# Laying Out Pages and Creating Long Documents

If text frames, graphics frames, lines, and shapes are the building blocks of layouts, then your InDesign documents are the architectural masterpieces you create with the building blocks. By setting up a solid framework using master pages, guidelines, and layers, and taking advantage of several long document features, you can quickly build a wide range of design-intensive multipage documents—from newsletters and newspapers to catalogs, magazines, and books.

In this chapter, you'll learn how to use master pages as backgrounds for document pages and how to use several different kinds of guidelines to place and align objects on pages. You'll also learn how to use layers to organize objects within documents. Additionally, we explain how to add, move, and delete pages in a multipage document and how to take advantage of several features for working with and organizing long documents.

# #79 Working with Master Pages

If you use InDesign to create long documents, such as books, catalogs, magazines, and newspapers, understanding and using master pages is critical to working efficiently. A master page serves as the background for document pages and contains elements that appear on all pages, like page numbers, page headers, and page footers. A master page can also contain placeholder frames for text and graphics. Placing objects on master pages and basing document pages on master pages saves you the time and effort required to manually place repeated elements on multiple document pages.

When you create a new document, it contains a single blank master page called A-Master. For facing-page documents, A-Master has a left (verso) page and a right (recto) page. By default, all document pages are based on A-Master. Objects that you place on A-Master are automatically placed on document pages based on A-Master.

The Pages palette (Window > Pages; **Figure 79a**) displays thumbnails of master pages (top) and document pages (below). To display a master page in the document window, double-click a master page thumbnail. Use InDesign's drawing tools to add objects to master pages the same way you do for document pages. Objects you place on a left-side master page in a facing-page document are placed on even-numbered pages; objects you place on a right-side master page are placed on odd-numbered pages. Master objects are placed at the bottom of the layer they're on—at the bottom of the stacking order (see #82 for more information about layers). If you want to place master objects in front of objects on document pages, create a layer for them and make it the topmost layer.

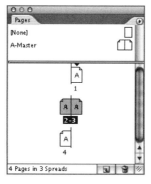

**Figure 79a** Master page thumbnails are displayed at the top of the Pages palette. Document page thumbnails are below.

You can create and use as many master pages as you want. For example, a newsletter might have a master page that's based on a three-column format and another that's based on a two-column format. When laying out the newsletter, you can base its pages on either the three-column or two-column master page.

To create a new master page, choose New Master from the Pages palette menu. In the New Master dialog box (**Figure 79b**) assign a prefix and a name. The Based on Master menu lets you base a new master page on an existing master page to create a parent-child-type relationship between the two. Changes you make to the parent master page are automatically applied to the child master. For a facing-page document, the Number of Pages should be 2 (left side and right side).

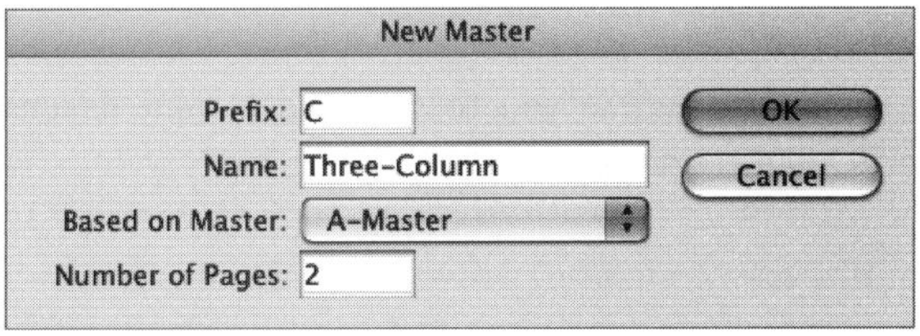

Figure 79b When you create a new master page, you can assign a prefix and a name, and choose another master page as its "parent."

You can apply a master page to a document page in several ways:

- Drag a master page thumbnail onto a document page thumbnail. If you drag a master page thumbnail onto the dog-eared corner of a facing-page document page, a black border is displayed around the spread. Release the mouse to apply the master page to both pages of the spread.

- Select one or more document page thumbnails, choose Apply Master to Pages from the Pages palette menu, and then choose a master page from the Apply Master menu.

- If you choose Insert pages from the Pages palette menu to add pages to a document, you can assign a master page for the new pages by choosing one from the Master menu in the Insert Pages dialog box.

**The "None" Master Page**

In addition to the A-Master master page, all documents include a master page called None. The None master page is completely blank—no margins, columns, or objects—and you can't modify it. You can use the None master page for blank document pages. For example, if you're laying out a magazine, you could use the None master page as a placeholder for document pages that will contain full-page ads.

## Selecting and Modifying Master Objects on Document Pages

The objects you place on a master page are referred to as *master objects*. You can't select a master object on a document page by simply clicking it with a selection tool as you do with nonmaster objects. To select a master object on a document page, press Command+Shift (Mac OS) or Ctrl+Shift (Windows) and click the object with a selection tool. If you make a change to a master object on a document page, it remains a master object, and subsequent changes you make to the object on the master page are applied to the master object you modified on the document page. To break a link between a master object on a document page and its master page, select the object on the document page, and then choose Detach Selection From Master from the Pages palette menu.

When you change a document page's master page, the margins, columns, and objects from the old master page are removed from the document page, and the margins, columns, and objects on the new master page are added. When you change an object on a master page, the change is reflected on all pages based on that master page.

The Pages palette menu includes several commands for working with master pages. Here's a brief description of a few that are particularly useful:

- **Override All Master Page Items** allows you to make local changes to a master object on a document page and still maintain a link to the object on the master page.

- **Undo All Local Overrides** allows you to undo any changes you've made to master objects on a document page.

- **Detach All Objects from Master** allows you to break the link between master objects on the current page and its master page.

- **Save as Master** allows you to save the current document page as a master page.

# #80 Setting Margins and Columns

When you create a new document, you can specify the number of columns, the gutter width between columns, and a margin for each page edge. Column and margin settings are used to display guidelines that help you position text frames, graphic frames, and other elements on pages. The settings you specify in the New Document dialog box are used for all document pages unless you change the column and margin settings for the document's master page, or you change the settings for individual document pages.

Before you can change column and margin settings for a master page or specific document pages, you must first select—or *target*—the pages you want to change in the Pages palette. To target both pages of a facing-page master page, click the name of the master page. To target only the verso or recto page of a facing-page master page, click the left or right master page thumbnail. To target a document page, click its thumbnail. To target a range of documents or master pages, click the thumbnail of the first page, and then Shift-click the thumbnail of the last page. Command-click (Mac OS) or Ctrl-click (Windows) to select multiple, nonsequential master or document pages.

After you've targeted the pages whose column and margin settings you want to change, choose Layout > Margins and Columns. In the Margins and Columns dialog box (**Figure 80**), change the margin and column settings.

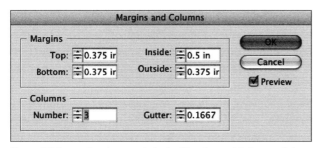

Figure 80 The settings you apply in the Margins and Columns dialog box are applied to the pages targeted in the Pages palette.

If you change the settings in the Margins and Columns dialog box when no documents are open, the modified settings become the default settings used in the New Document dialog box.

## Showing and Hiding Margin and Column Guides

To turn off the display of margin and column guides, choose View > Grids & Guides > Hide Guides. You can also hide all guidelines by clicking the Preview button in the toolbox.

## Margins, Bleeds, and Printing

It's easy to confuse the margin guides with the outside edge of a page or spread. Margin guides are displayed in color, whereas page edges are black. You'll probably place most elements within the margin guides, but there's no restriction on placing objects between the margin guides and the edge of the page. Objects that extend beyond the edge of the page are referred to as *bleed objects.* Most desktop printers cannot print to the edge of the page, which means that bleed objects get clipped.

# #81 Using Guides and Grids

If you like to use guidelines when you lay out pages, you may need more than margin and column guides. If that's the case, you can use ruler guides, a document-wide grid, or a combination of both. For example, you can quickly divide a page into quadrants by adding a vertical ruler guide and a horizontal ruler guide that intersect at the center of the page. Or you can use a document-wide baseline grid for aligning text and objects across columns. While it's nice to have so many options when it comes to adding guidelines, you probably won't use them all.

Ruler guides and grids are similar in that they don't print (unless you want to print them), and they help you align objects. They're also different in some ways:

- **Ruler guides** are much like objects. You can select them with the Selection tools, move, and delete them, and they're layer specific. Ruler guides can be vertical or horizontal only.

- **Gridlines** are document-wide and cannot be selected or modified.

You can create ruler guides in two ways: manually by clicking and dragging a ruler or automatically using the Create Guides command (Layout menu).

- **To create a ruler guide manually,** click the ruler along the left or top edge of the document window and drag the pointer onto a page or the pasteboard. (Choose View > Show Rulers if the rulers are not showing.) If you click the vertical ruler along the left edge of the document window, you create a vertical ruler guide. If you click the horizontal ruler at the top of the document window, you create a horizontal ruler guide. Release the mouse when the pointer is on a page to create a page guide that spans the page. Release the mouse when the pointer is on the pasteboard to create a spread guide that spans the page or spread and pasteboard.

## Snapping Objects to Guides and Grids

If the Snap to Guides and Snap to Document Grid commands (View > Grids & Guides) are checked, object edges and centerpoints will snap to ruler guides and gridlines, respectively, when you drag objects near them. The Snap to Zone value in the Guides & Pasteboard panel in the Preferences dialog box determines the distance at which an object will snap to a ruler guide or gridline.

Laying Out Pages and Creating Long Documents

- **To create ruler guides automatically,** select the document or master pages to which you want to add guides in the Pages palette, and then choose Layout > Create Guides. The controls in the Create Guides dialog box (**Figure 81a**) let you create horizontal guides (Rows), vertical ruler guides (Columns), or both. If you don't specify a Gutter value, a single guide is placed for each row/column. If you specify a Gutter value, it's used as the space between a pair of ruler guides. Other options let you fit the guides within the margins or the page and remove existing ruler guides.

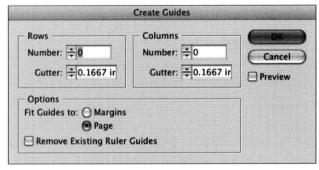

Figure 81a Use the controls in the Create Guides dialog box to divide a page into rows and columns using ruler guides.

Regardless of the method you use to create ruler guides, you can select, move, and delete them just like objects. You can also copy ruler guides into a Library and between pages.

If you like to use a grid when you lay out pages, InDesign offers two options:

- **A baseline grid** is a set of evenly spaced horizontal lines that help align text and objects across multiple columns.

- **A document grid** is a set of evenly spaced horizontal and vertical lines that resembles graph paper.

## Text Frame-specific Baseline Grids

A new feature in InDesign CS2 lets you add a baseline grid to individual text frames. A frame-based baseline grid makes it easy to align baselines of text across multiple columns within a frame. To add a baseline grid to a text frame, select the frame, and then choose Object > Text Frame Options. Use the controls in the Baseline Options panel in the Text Frame Options dialog box to control the placement of the gridlines. The Show/Hide Baseline Grid command (View > Grids & Guides) controls the display of frame-based baseline grids.

The Baseline Grid controls in the Grids panel in the Preferences dialog box (**Figure 81b**) let you modify a document's baseline grid. You can specify the Color, Start point, Increment, and View Threshold. The Show/Hide Baseline Grid command (View > Grids & Guides) lets you control the display of the baseline grid. (Note: The Align to Baseline Grid button in the Paragraph palette let's you align the baselines of selected paragraphs to the baseline grid.)

The Document Grid controls let you modify the document grid. You can specify Color as well as increments (Gridline Every) and subincrements (Subdivisions) for Horizontal and Vertical lines. The Show/Hide Document Grid command (View > Grids & Guides) lets you control the display of the document grid.

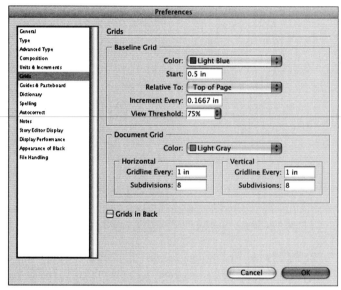

**Figure 81b** Use the controls in the Grids panel in the Preferences dialog box to modify a document's baseline grid and document grid.

# #**82** Working with Layers

By default, every time you create a new document, it contains a single layer named "Layer 1." Each new object you create occupies a successively higher position in the layer's stacking order. If you want, you can create additional layers, and then use them for organizing objects. For example, you could create one layer called "Text" and use it for all of the text frames in a document and another layer called "Graphics" that holds all graphic elements. You could then show, hide, or print each layer individually or both layers together.

To create a new layer, open the Layers palette (Window > Layers), and then choose New Layer from the palette menu. In the New Layer dialog box (**Figure 82a**), enter a Name for the layer and use the controls to specify layer attributes.

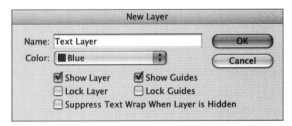

**Figure 82a** Use the controls in the New Layer dialog box to specify attributes of a new layer.

After you create a new layer, it's displayed in the Layers palette (**Figure 82b**) as the topmost layer in the list, which means it's the topmost layer in the layer stacking order. It's also the selected layer, indicated by the Pen icon. The small, square icon to the right of the Pen icon indicates the layer of the selected object. New objects you create with the drawing tools are placed on the selected layer. If you want to add new objects to a different layer, select the layer in the palette, and then add the objects.

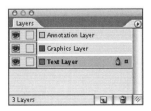

**Figure 82b** The Layers palette displays a list of a document's layers and includes controls and commands for working with layers.

## Paste Remembers Layers

If you check Paste Remembers Layers in the Layers palette menu, objects you cut or copy retain their layer when you choose Edit > Paste. If you paste objects into a different document, layer names are also copied and added to the Layers palette if they don't exist in the target document. If Paste Remembers Layers is unchecked, all cut or copied objects are pasted onto the selected layer.

Two buttons are displayed to the left of each layer's name:

- Click the button on the left to alternately show and hide a layer.

- Click the button on the right to alternately lock or unlock a layer. You can't select objects on locked layers.

You can also use the controls in the Layers palette to:

- **Delete layers** by selecting them, and then clicking the Delete (Trash) button.

- **Rearrange layers** by dragging selected layers up or down within the list. The layer at the bottom of the list is the lowest layer in the stacking order.

- **Change the layer of the selected object** by dragging the small square on the right side of the palette to a new layer. If nothing is selected, the square is not displayed.

The Layers palette contains additional commands for working with layers, including Delete, Hide Others, Lock Others, Merge, and Delete Unused Layers.

Some other details you should know about layers:

- If you create a group that contains objects that are on different layers, all objects are moved to the layer of the topmost object and placed consecutively in the stacking order.

- If you place an object on a master page, it's placed at the bottom of the stacking order of the selected layer. If you want a master object to be placed in front of other objects, put it on a layer that's in front of the object's layer.

# #**83** Working with Pages

When you create a new document, the value you enter in the Number of Pages field in the New Document dialog box determines how many pages the document has; however, you're free to change your mind later on and add or delete pages as needed. You can also move pages within a document.

The Pages palette (Window > Pages; **Figure 83a**) provides the easiest method for working with the pages in a multipage document. The thumbnails at the top of the palette represent a document's master pages; the thumbnails at the bottom of the palette represent document pages. (For more information about master pages, see #79.)

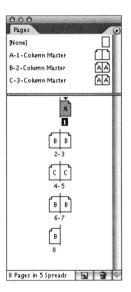

Figure 83a The Pages palette displays thumbnails of master pages (top) and document pages (bottom), and includes controls and commands for working with pages.

### Keeping a Facing-page Spread Together

If you design a facing-page spread and you want to make sure that the two pages are not separated if pages are added, deleted, or moved, select both thumbnails in the Pages palette, and then choose Keep Spread Together from the palette menu.

## Creating a Multipage Spread

Some publications contain fold-out pages that open into three-page spreads called *gatefolds*. To create a multipage spread in InDesign, select a spread in the Pages palette, choose Keep Spread Together, and then insert a new page immediately before or after the spread. Generally, you create a gatefold by adding an extra page to the right side of a facing-page spread, and then adding an extra page to the left side of the next facing-page spread.

You can add pages to a document in several ways:

- **To add a single page,** click the Create New Page button at the bottom of the Pages palette. The new page is placed after the page that's currently displayed in the document window—or at the end of the document if a master page is currently displayed—and uses the master page of the preceding page.

- **To add a page based on a particular master page,** drag a master page thumbnail from the top of the palette to the bottom of the palette. To control where the new page is placed, drag the thumbnail to the left or the right edge of a document page. A vertical bar is displayed to indicate where the page will be placed. (If you release the mouse when a page icon is highlighted, you'll apply the selected master to the document page.) Drag the thumbnail just above or below document page thumbnails to place the new page between the pages. If you select both the left and right thumbnails of a facing-page master page before dragging, two pages are inserted.

- **To add one or more pages,** choose Insert Pages from the Pages palette menu. The Insert Pages dialog box (**Figure 83b**) includes controls for specifying the number of pages to insert, where they're placed, and which master page they're based on.

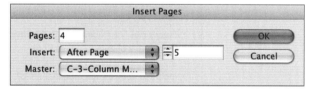

**Figure 83b** When you choose Insert Pages from the Pages palette menu, the Insert pages dialog box lets you specify the number of pages to add, where to place them, and which master page they're based on.

A document can contain as many as 9,999 pages, although you wouldn't want to create such a large document. If you need to create a long document, it's often a good idea to use InDesign's book feature to organize it as several smaller documents. For more about creating books, see #85.

Although it's easy to move pages within a document, you should do so with great care. If a document contains facing-page spreads that were designed as a pair, moving a single page can split them. To move a page, select its thumbnail in the Pages palette and drag it elsewhere. As you drag the thumbnail, a vertical bar is displayed when it's next to a page edge to indicate where the page will be placed. If you drag the thumbnail between page icons, an arrow indicates how the pages will be pushed apart to accommodate the moved page.

To delete a page, click its thumbnail in the Pages palette, and then click the Delete (Trash) button. Command-click (Mac OS) or Ctrl-click (Windows) to select multiple, nonsequential pages. Click a thumbnail, and then Shift-click another thumbnail to select a range of pages.

The Pages palette menu includes several more commands for working with documents, master pages, and spreads. Before you choose a command in the Pages palette, you should select the thumbnails of the pages you want to work with. The commands vary depending on whether a single page, a single spread, multiple pages, or multiple spreads are selected in the palette.

The Layout > Pages menu also includes several commands for working with pages, including Add Page, Insert Pages, Move Pages, and Apply Master to Pages.

For information about navigating within a multipage document, see #15.

## Copying Pages Between Documents

You can copy pages between two open documents by displaying the document windows side by side (choose Window > Arrange > Tile to arrange document windows), selecting the thumbnails of the pages you want to copy in the Pages palette, and then dragging and dropping the page icon within the other document window. Copied pages are placed at the end of the target document. When you copy pages between documents, character and paragraph styles, colors, layers, and master pages are also copied.

# #84 Numbering Pages and Creating Sections

Since publications are not always numbered from page 1 to the end—and since each InDesign document doesn't necessarily contain an entire publication—you have complete control over the format, placement, and starting number for automatic page numbering. A book, for example, might start out with Roman numerals (i–xvi) for the front matter and then use standard numerals (1–64) for the chapters. A textbook might preface each page number with a letter and start each chapter on page one (A.1–A.24, B.1–B.36, etc.). A range of pages in a document with different page numbering—the front matter, for example—is referred to as a *section*.

To get started with page numbers, you first need to insert the Auto Page Number character in text. Then you can use the Section options to customize it.

## Inserting the Auto Page Number Character

Generally, you will place the Auto Page Number character on a master page. That way, all pages based on that page will have a page number. However, you can insert the Auto Page Number Character on any page, in any location, and it will display the appropriate page number. If you reorder pages, the page numbers update as well. To insert the Auto Page Number character:

1. Select the Type tool.

2. Click in a text frame or on a type path (usually on a master page).

3. Choose Type > Insert > Insert Special Character > Auto Page Number.

4. If you're on a master page, a placeholder displays. The placeholder is the same as the letter prefacing the master page name (that is, B-Master's Auto Page Number placeholder is a "B"). If you're on a document page, the appropriate page number displays.

5. Highlight the page number or placeholder and use the Character pane in the Control palette or the Character palette (Type menu) to format it (**Figure 84a**).

Laying Out Pages and Creating Long Documents

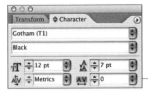

**B** DECEMBER 2005 / JANUARY 2006

**Figure 84a** Adding the Auto Page Number character to master page B-Master results in the placeholder character "B." Formatting the highlighted "B" indicates the character formatting you want for the page numbers.

## Creating Sections

While the look of page numbers depends on character formats you apply to the Auto Page Number character, all other attributes of page numbers comes from the New Section or Numbering & Section Options dialog box. To use Roman numerals, begin a document on a different page number, include a preface with page numbers, and more, you need to create a section. A section of automatic page numbering will continue through a document until you create a new section (**Figure 84b**).

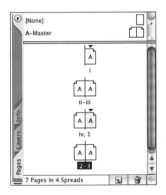

**Figure 84b** In this document, the first four pages have Roman numerals i–iv. A new section starts on the fifth page of the document, but starts the numbering at 1 and uses Arabic numerals.

To create a section:

1. In the Pages palette, click the page you want to be the first page in the section.

2. Choose Numbering & Section Options from the Layout menu or the Pages palette menu. The New Section dialog box displays (**Figure 84c**); if a section already starts on the selected page, the Numbering & Section Options dialog box displays.

3. Check Start Section. (This is unavailable if you've selected the first page of the document.)

4. To specify a starting page number, click Start Page Numbering At and enter the page number in the field. To pick up the page numbering where the last section left off, click Automatic Page Numbering.

5. If you want to include a prefix for page numbers—such as "Chapter 1-" or "Index"—enter that text in the Section Prefix field. To separate the prefix text from the page number, be sure to include a space or other separation character after the text in the Section Prefix field.

6. By default, the prefix text shows with the page number at the bottom of the document window. To actually add the prefix text to the page numbers on the page, check Include Prefix When Numbering Pages.

For information about the Section Marker field, read on.

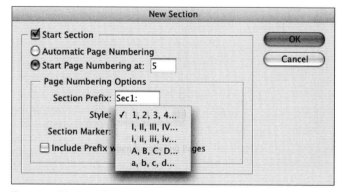

**Figure 84c** The New Section dialog box lets you specify the starting page number, the type of numerals to use, and the page number prefix for a section of pages.

## Using Section Markers

In addition to having specific page numbers, sections can have *section marker* text that you can insert on any page. For example, if you have a section for each chapter in a book, the marker for each section might be the chapter name. If you then put the section marker at the top of the master page, the pages in each section will always show the correct chapter name—even if you pick up pages and move them to a different chapter.

To use a section marker:

1. Enter the text for it in the Section Marker field in the New Section or Numbering & Section Options dialog box.

2. Select the Type tool.

3. Click in a text frame or on a type path (usually on a master page).

4. Choose Type > Insert > Insert Special Character > Section Marker.

# #85 Creating a Book

When working on longer publications such as magazine and books, it's common to separate the content into multiple documents such as one document per article or one document per chapter. This allows multiple people to work on different parts of the publication, and it keeps the file sizes small, which results in files that open and save faster. To manage multiple documents for the same publication—including updating page numbers across documents and making sure styles remain consistent—InDesign provides *book* files. A book actually displays as a palette, which serves as a container for the documents that make up the publication.

## Creating a Book File

A book is another type of InDesign file, recognized by its file extension of .indb. Before you create a book file, however, it's helpful to get your project organized. Create a folder for the project and place all the documents for the book in it. (You do not need to have all the documents ready—you can add documents to a book at any time.) The project folder is also a good place to store any templates, libraries, graphics, and fonts for the project. To create a book:

1. Choose File > New > Book.

2. In the New Book dialog box, enter a name for the book in the Save As field.

3. Navigate to the folder containing the documents for the book; you can save the book in another location, but it's easiest to keep track of the files if you store the book and its documents in the same folder.

4. Click Save. The book palette opens with the name of the book in a tab.

## Opening and Closing a Book

You can open the book like you open any other file—choose File > Open or double-click a book file icon on the desktop. If multiple books are open, additional tabs display in the Book palette. You can tear off these tabs to create individual palettes for each book.

To close a book, click the palette's close button or choose Close Book from the Book palette menu. You will be prompted to save changes to the book (such as adding or rearranging documents) before you close the book.

**Note**

*A book does not have to remain open while you work on its documents.*

**Saving Books**

Changes made to a book, such as adding documents, are not saved automatically. To save changes, choose Save Book from the Book palette menu.

## Adding Documents

When you first create a book, it is empty and waiting for you to add documents. You can add up to 1,000 documents to a book, and a single document can be included in multiple books. To add documents to a book:

**1.** Click the Add Documents button at the bottom of the Book palette (**Figure 85a**) or choose Add Document from the Book palette menu.

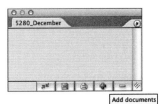

**Figure 85a** The Add Documents button lets you select the InDesign documents to include in a book.

**2.** Select the document you want to add to the book. If multiple documents are in the same folder, you can add them all at once. Command-click (Mac OS) or Ctrl-click to select multiple documents, or Shift-click to select a continuous range of documents.

**3.** Click Open to add the documents.

**4.** You may see alerts regarding missing fonts, but you can click OK to bypass these for the purposes of adding the documents to the book. (Later, for accurate page numbering, you need to be sure no fonts are missing.)

You can also add documents to a book by dragging InDesign files from the desktop into the book.

## Working with Books

Once documents are in a book, you can open them through the book for editing, rearrange documents in a book, replace documents with different ones, and remove documents from a book.

- **To open a document for editing,** open its book. Then double-click the document name in the Book palette.

- **To replace a document in a book,** select the document in the book and choose Replace Document from the Book palette menu.

- **To remove a document from a book,** select it and click the Remove Documents button  at the bottom of the Book palette or choose Remove Document from the palette menu.

- **To rearrange the documents in the book,** click a document name and drag it up or down within the list (**Figure 85b**). If you're using automatic page numbering within the book, the page numbers update when you reorder chapters.

**Figure 85b** You can drag a document to a new location within a book.

## Synchronizing Book Styles

To make sure that all the documents that make up a book remain consistent, you can synchronize styles, including object styles, paragraph styles, character styles, and color swatches. This way, if you modify a style or add one, the change can be automatically implemented in the entire book. You can synchronize all the documents in a book or selected documents. To synchronize:

1. Determine which document has the "right" styles that you want in all the documents. (For example, if you want to make a global change in a paragraph style, be sure the document you make the change in has all the appropriate styles in it.)

2. Click to the left of that document name in the Book palette. The Tool Tip will display "Indicates the Style Source" for that document.

3. Select the documents in the book that you want to synchronize. To synchronize the entire book, click in the blank area at the bottom of the palette to deselect all the documents.

4. Click Synchronize 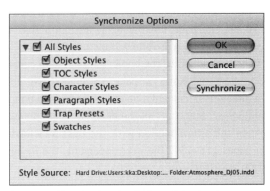 at the bottom of the Book palette or choose Synchronize Selected Documents from the palette menu.

5. An alert regarding missing fonts may display, but you can click OK to bypass this alert for synchronization purposes.

6. InDesign opens each document, makes the changes, saves it, and closes it. Therefore, you *cannot* undo synchronization.

To customize this feature, you can specify which styles synchronize by choosing Synchronize Options from the Book palette menu. Check the styles you want to synchronize in the Synchronize Options dialog box (**Figure 85c**). At this point, you can click the Synchronize button to synchronize all the documents in the book.

**Figure 85c** The Synchronize Options dialog box lets you customize which styles synchronize.

# #86 Paginating a Book

One advantage of using a book to manage multiple documents is the ability to use automatic pagination. As you work on documents in a book, adding and removing pages, InDesign can update page numbers throughout all the documents. In addition, if you want all the documents to start on a left-facing (even-numbered) or right-facing (odd-numbered) page, InDesign can automatically insert pages at the end of one document to ensure that the next document starts on the correct facing page.

By default, the book is paginated the same way the documents are. So if the documents use automatic page numbering and all start on page 1, the book is numbered sequentially from the first page of the first document to the last page of the last document. If there are any sections of page numbers created within a document, those are reflected in the book. Whenever a section is started, it follows through the documents in a book until InDesign encounters another section start.

For example, the first document in this book (**Figure 86a**) is the Cover, and it has the page number of 1, although that will not display anywhere. The cover is followed by a series of ads in a document that is not yet added to the book. The second document, TOC, has a section start and starts on page 8. The next two documents follow the previous document's page numbering, so you see 8–11, 12–33, and 34–37. Since not all the documents are ready for this book, you then see a new section with the Best New Restaurants feature on pages 118–129. The next document, the Reviews, follows the feature and starts on page 130.

**Figure 86a** Books can have many sections of page numbers.

To specify how page numbering works for a book, choose Book Page Numbering Options from the Book palette menu. In the Page Order area (**Figure 86b**), specify how each document should start:

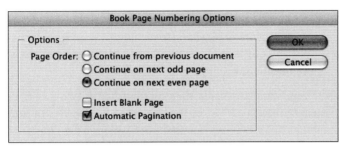

**Figure 86b** The Book Page Numbering Options dialog box helps you ensure that pages are numbered correctly from document to document.

- **Continue From Previous Document** starts the page numbering according to the last page of the previous document. If the document ends on page 10, the next document starts on page 11. If the document ends on page 11, the next document starts on page 12. This setting is appropriate for single-sided documents.

- **Continue on Next Odd Page** always starts the page numbering of a document on an odd (right-facing) page. If a document ends on page 11, the next document starts on page 13. This setting might be appropriate for chapters of a book, which usually start on a right-facing page.

- **Continue on Next Even Page** always starts the page numbering of a document on an even (left-facing) page. If a document ends on page 12, the next document starts on page 14. This setting might be appropriate for a magazine in which each document is a feature that starts on a left-facing page.

*(continued on next page)*

## Paginating Requires Documents and Fonts

To accurately paginate a document, InDesign needs to open each document, look at the number of pages it currently has, determine whether to add any pages to the end, and then close it. Therefore, if a document is open by another user or missing from its original location, you cannot accurately paginate. In addition, if fonts for a document are missing, InDesign cannot determine if the text is flowing properly, and therefore it cannot determine if the document has the correct amount of pages. For accurate pagination, be sure all the fonts used in the book are active on your computer.

- **To insert blank pages at the ends of chapters,** click Continue on Next Odd Page or Continue on Next Even Page and InDesign will insert the blank pages. So, if a document ends on page 12 but the next document has to start on page 14, this will automatically insert a blank page 13 at the end of the document. To do this, check Insert Blank Page.

- **Check Automatic Pagination** to continually repaginate the book as you work on chapters. If you prefer to wait until the book is more final, you can uncheck this option and choose Repaginate from the Book palette menu any time you want to update the pagination.

If you want to change the page numbering of an individual document in a book, select the document and choose Document Page Numbering Options from the Book palette menu. (As a shortcut, you can double-click the document's page numbers shown in the Book palette.) The controls in the Document Page Numbering Options dialog box are explained in #84. If you create a section for a document, that page numbering is followed through the documents in the book until another section start is encountered.

# #**87** Inserting Footnotes

If you need to insert footnotes in text, InDesign can automatically format the footnote reference number, place and format the footnote text, and update the footnotes as text changes and footnotes are added. You have complete control over the text formatting and layout, so you decide precisely how footnotes look. This takes working with footnotes from being a potentially tedious and time-consuming task to an almost effortless process.

To insert a footnote:

1. Click anywhere in text using the Type tool.

2. Choose Type > Insert Footnote. A footnote reference number is automatically inserted, and the flashing text insertion bar is placed at the bottom of the column, ready for you to type the footnote text (**Figure 87a**).

3. Enter or paste the footnote text, and then choose Type > Go to Footnote Reference to return to the main text.

If text reflows, the footnote will move with its reference text as necessary.

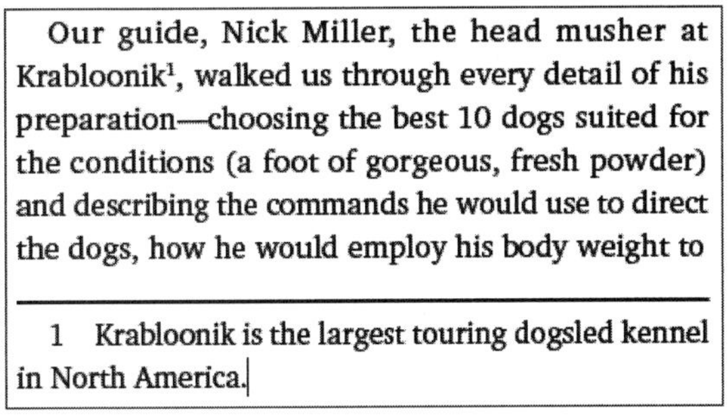

> Our guide, Nick Miller, the head musher at Krabloonik[1], walked us through every detail of his preparation—choosing the best 10 dogs suited for the conditions (a foot of gorgeous, fresh powder) and describing the commands he would use to direct the dogs, how he would employ his body weight to
>
> ---
>
> 1   Krabloonik is the largest touring dogsled kennel in North America.

**Figure 87a** A footnote is inserted next to "Krabloonik" in the second line of the paragraph. Then, for the footnote text, a definition of "Krabloonik" was typed in.

## Importing Footnotes from Word

If you import text from Microsoft Word that has footnotes, you can import and place the footnotes automatically. To do this, click Show Import Options in the Place dialog box, and then check Footnotes. The footnote reference numbers and text are imported from Word but formatted and placed according to settings in the Footnote Options dialog box.

Footnotes generally look the same throughout an entire document. Therefore, the controls for specifying the text formatting and placement of footnotes work for all the footnotes in a document, not for individual footnotes. You can change the formatting at any time, but to prevent a lot of text reflow, you may want to set up the footnote formatting before you start inserting footnotes. To format footnotes, choose Type > Document Footnote Options.

Use the Numbering and Formatting panel (**Figure 87b**) to specify how footnotes are numbered, the formatting of the footnote reference in text, and the formatting of the actual footnote text.

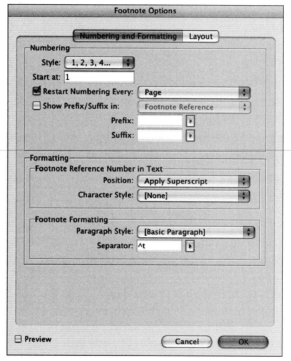

**Figure 87b** In the Numbering and Formatting panel, you can select a character style for footnote reference numbers and a paragraph style for footnote text, among many other formatting options.

Use the Layout panel (**Figure 87c**) to control how footnotes are placed on the page, including the amount of space before and between footnotes, and how footnotes are handled if the text is too long. If you want to place a rule above footnotes, you can specify its usage and formatting.

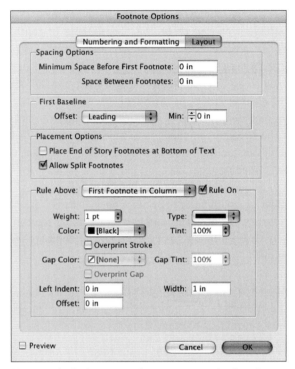

**Figure 87c** In the Layout panel, you can customize the rule above footnotes and how footnotes are placed on the page.

# #**88** Creating Tables of Contents

Creating and updating a table of contents, especially for a long book, can be a chore. The names of heads and subheads change, page numbers change, chapter order changes—so you're constantly modifying what's supposed to be the "final" table of contents. Then there's the proofreading, making sure all the text and page numbers actually match the final content. Fortunately, there's an automatic way to do this, provided that you use paragraph styles to format the chapter names, heads, subheads, and other text that will become part of the table of contents. InDesign can extract the text in those paragraph styles, and then produce and update a richly formatted table of contents for a single document or a book—no proofreading required.

Note that although the feature is called "table of contents," it's useful for creating any type of list from a document. For example, you might create a list of images or charts for a book. You can, in fact, create as many different types of "tables of contents" for a book as you need.

## Preparing for a Table of Contents

Creating a table of contents requires a little preparation and planning. Here are a few steps to start with:

1. Figure out what text you want in the table of contents, such as chapter heads, section heads, and subheads.

2. Determine which paragraph styles are applied to that text. (If necessary, make sure the paragraph styles are applied consistently throughout the documents—if not, text may be left out.)

3. Decide how you want the table of contents to look, including the title of the table of contents, the text formatting, and the placement and look of page numbers.

4. Create paragraph and character styles for the table of contents, including its title, each level of text (chapters names, section heads, etc.), and page numbers. If you're going to use a tab to separate each table of contents entry from its page number, be sure to set that tab and specify any leader characters you want (such as ...) in the paragraph style.

5. Create a placeholder for the table of contents—either blank pages in a document or a blank document in a book. If the table of contents will have a special design, create a master page for it as well.

As an example, this craft book has a main table of contents for the entire book and a mini-table of contents for each chapter (**Figure 88a**). Some of the formatting, such as the bullets and the bracket under the chapter name, are on the master page. The text consists of the chapter name, "Backyard Botanicals," the craft names followed by a tab, a bracket, and the page number. In the formatted table of contents, the chapter name is centered in 27-point Baskerville Old Face font; the craft names are deeply indented, 12-point Syntax; and the page numbers are 11-point Helvetica Neue Medium Italic.

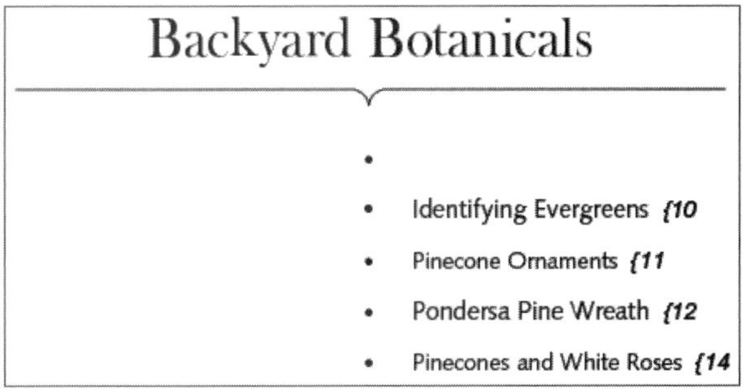

### Importing Tables of Contents from Word

If you import text from Microsoft Word that has a table of contents, the entries and page numbers can be imported as well. However, the page numbers may not be accurate after the text is flowed into the InDesign document, and there is no way to update them. You may be better off not importing the table of contents. To do this, click Show Import Options in the Place dialog box, and then uncheck Table of Contents Text in the Include area.

## Backyard Botanicals

- 
- Identifying Evergreens {10
- Pinecone Ornaments {11
- Pondersa Pine Wreath {12
- Pinecones and White Roses {14

**Figure 88a** InDesign can create richly formatted tables of contents such as this one.

## Generating a Table of Contents

Once you've prepared by identifying the text you want in the table of contents and creating paragraph and character styles for it, choose Layout > Table of Contents. In the Table of Contents dialog box, you can specify the styles used to create the table of contents or list, how it should be formatted, and more.

- **Title area:** If you want to place a heading on the table of contents (such as "Contents" or "Figures List"), enter the text in the Title field. To specify the formatting of the title, choose an option from the Style menu at right.

- **Styles in Table of Contents area:** This is where you specify what text goes into the table of contents. In the Other Styles list at left, locate the paragraph style applied to the first level of head that will go in the table of contents—such as Chapter Head. Select it in the list and click Add. Then select the paragraph style applied to the second level of head and click Add. Continue adding paragraph styles in order until you've added all the styles that should appear in the table of contents. Be sure to add the styles according to the hierarchy of information, such as Chapter Heads, Section Heads, Subheads, etc.

- **Style area:** To specify the formatting for the table of contents, click the first paragraph style in the Include Paragraph Styles list. Then choose a paragraph style from the Style menu below. For example, you might map the Chapter Head paragraph style to the TOC Level 1 paragraph style.

- **More Options button:** To further fine-tune the formatting for each table of contents entry, click More Options. In the Style area, you can specify where page numbers are placed (such as before or after the text) and how they are separated from the entries (such as with an em space or tab). You can also choose character styles for the page numbers and separation characters. In this same area, you can specify that the entries are alphabetized and change the level of information. All the controls in the Style area are specific to the paragraph style selected in the Include Paragraph Styles area; therefore, you may need to set these options for each included style.

- **Options area:** To produce a table of contents for an entire book, check Include Book Documents. Other options in this area let you automatically create PDF bookmarks for table of contents entries, replace an existing table of contents, create a "run-in" table of contents (with semicolons rather than paragraph returns separating entries), and specify whether to include text on layers that are hidden.

Once you're finished setting up the table of contents, click OK in the Table of Contents dialog box (**Figure 88b**). InDesign looks through the document or book, finds all the text, formats it, and then loads the cursor with the fully formatted table of contents. Flow the text into a text frame as you usually would.

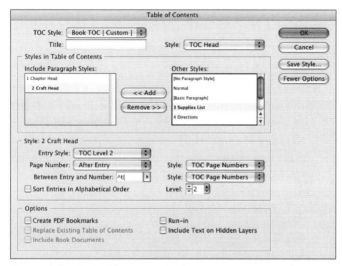

**Figure 88b** The Table of Contents dialog box lets you specify what text goes into a table of contents and precisely how it should look. To make the table of contents shown in Figure 88a, the paragraph style "2 Craft Head" is mapped to "TOC Level 2" and separated from its page number with a tab and a right-facing bracket. Both the page number and bracket are formatted with a character style called "TOC Page Numbers."

Don't be surprised if it's not perfect the first time. With all the detailed settings, you might miss a paragraph style or forget to select the character style for the page numbers. But don't be tempted to manually touch up the table of contents. For one thing, manual changes will not be reflected if you created PDF bookmarks. For another, you will inevitably end up making those manual changes more than once. No matter how "final" you think the document or book is, you usually end up generating the table of contents several times. Generating the table of contents is fairly quick, even for a long book, so you can whip one up just to see how many pages you need or to see if you got all the settings right. Then update it as often as needed.

## Creating a Table of Contents for a Book

If you're creating a table of contents for a book, follow these steps:

1. Be sure all the documents in the book are available (not missing or open by another user).

2. Make sure all the fonts are active. If text is reflowing due to missing fonts, the page numbers may not be accurate.

3. Choose Repaginate from the Book palette menu before you create the table of contents.

4. Create the table of contents for the book in a document that will contain it. The document must contain all the necessary paragraph and character styles for creating and formatting the table of contents. If necessary, synchronize the book to make sure all the necessary styles are in that document. See #85 for more information.

5. If the table of contents is in the first document in the book, you may want to run a "draft" version first to see how many pages it takes up. Then repaginate the book and update the table of contents. If, for example, you save one page for a table of contents and end up using 10 pages, all the page numbers listed in the table of contents will be wrong (unless the table of contents is in its own section of page numbers).

6. Check Include Book Documents in the Table of Contents dialog box when setting up the table of contents.

## Updating a Table of Contents

As you work on a document or book, the table of contents *does not* update automatically. You need to manually update it to reflect changes to text, page numbers, and so on by choosing Layout > Update Table of Contents. If Replace Existing Table of Contents is checked in the Table of Contents dialog box, an alert displays indicating a successful update. If the option is not checked, the loaded text icon displays, and you can flow the table of contents wherever you want.

# #**89** Exporting a Book for PDF or Print

An advantage to working with books rather than juggling multiple documents is that you can output all the documents in a book at once. This includes preflighting, collecting files for output, exporting to PDF, and printing. Before working with output options, be sure all the documents are available (not open by other users or missing), all the linked graphic files are available, and all the necessary fonts are active.

You can output selected documents in a book or all the documents. To work with all the documents, click in the blank area at the bottom of the Book palette to deselect all the documents. To select individual documents, Command-click (Mac OS) or Ctrl-click the document names; to select a continuous range of documents, use Shift-click. To access the output options for books, click the Book palette menu (**Figure 89**):

- **Preflight Book:** This checks the documents' fonts, images, colors, and more to make sure they're ready for output. See #94 for more information.

- **Package Book:** This submenu lets you choose Book For Print or Book For GoLive, and will collect all the necessary files, including documents, fonts, and linked images. See #94 for more information.

- **Export Book to PDF:** This lets you output all the selected documents in the book as a single PDF. If you checked Create PDF Bookmarks in the Table of Contents dialog box, the PDF will already have links in it. See #95 for more information.

- **Print Book:** This opens the Print dialog box so you can print a hard copy of the book. See #98 for more information about printing. In addition to choosing Print Book, you can click the Print the Book button 🖨 at the bottom of the Book palette.

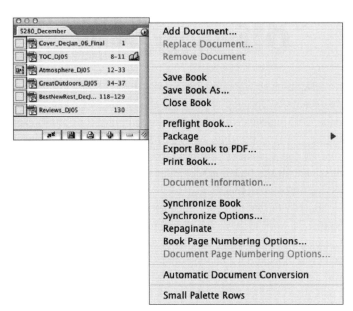

**Figure 89** The Book palette menu provides options for outputting all the documents in the book with the same settings. These include preflighting, collecting files for output, exporting the book to PDF, and printing the book.

Laying Out Pages and Creating Long Documents

# CHAPTER TEN

# Creating Media-rich PDFs

Over the past decade, Adobe's Portable Document Format (PDF) has become an important technology for both print and Web publishing. InDesign lets you export documents and books as PDF documents that can be used for a variety of purposes, from electronic distribution and onscreen review to high-resolution output. In addition to creating PDF documents that are intended to be printed, you can also create PDF documents that include hyperlinks, bookmarks, buttons, movies and sounds that are intended to be viewed onscreen.

In this chapter you'll learn how to add interactive elements to InDesign layouts that you will export as PDF, as well as how to add movies and sounds and control how they play in the exported PDF document.

# #90 Creating Hyperlinks

Because PDF documents can be opened and viewed onscreen, printed, or embedded into Web pages, they're somewhat of a hybrid. If you need to create a PDF that's intended primarily for onscreen display, you have the option of including hyperlinks that viewers can click to jump to other places within the document, other PDF documents, or Web sites.

To create a hyperlink, you have to specify two components: the *source*, which is the object or text that will act as the jumping-off point; and the *destination* to which the source points. The destination can be a page or a range of text within the document or another PDF document or a Web site.

To create a hyperlink destination to a page within an InDesign document you intend to export as PDF:

1. Choose Window > Interactive > Hyperlinks to open the Hyperlinks palette.

2. Choose New Hyperlink Destination from the palette menu.

3. In the New Hyperlink Destination dialog box (**Figure 90a**), choose Page from the Type menu. Other controls let you specify a name, choose a page, and select the Zoom Setting to display the destination page.

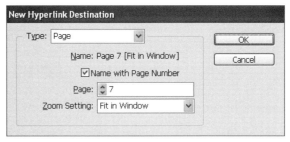

**Figure 90a** When you create a hyperlink destination, you can choose Page, Text Anchor, or URL from the Type menu. The controls displayed depend on the choice you make. Here you see the controls available for a Page destination.

To create a hyperlink that jumps to a range of text within a page, you must first create a text anchor to use as the hyperlink destination. To create a text anchor, click within text or select a range of text, and then choose New Hyperlink Destination from the Hyperlinks palette menu. You can use the default name in the Name field or assign a different name.

After you create hyperlink destinations, you're ready to create the source hyperlinks that jump to them. To create a new hyperlink:

1. Select an object or highlight a range of text, and then choose New Hyperlink from the Hyperlinks palette menu.

2. In the New Hyperlink dialog box (**Figure 90b**), use the default name in the Name field or change it.

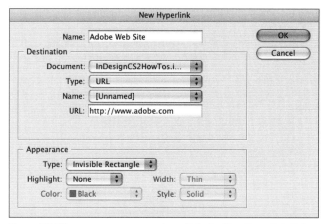

Figure 90b When you create a new hyperlink, the New Hyperlink dialog box lets you choose the destination and control the appearance of the hyperlink in the exported PDF document.

3. If you want to link to another PDF document, select it from the Document menu, which displays the names of open documents. You can choose Browse to select a document that's not open.

*(continued on next page)*

**#90**: Creating Hyperlinks

**4.** Choose Page, Anchor, or URL from the Type menu. The choice you make determines the controls that are displayed.

- If you choose Page, choose a page destination from the Name menu or specify a number in the Page field and choose a Zoom Setting.

- If you choose Text Anchor, choose a text anchor from the Name menu.

- If you choose URL, enter the URL in the URL field.

**5.** Use the controls in the Appearance area to specify how the hyperlink is displayed in the exported PDF document.

You can test a hyperlink by selecting it in the Hyperlinks palette, and then choosing Go To Destination from the palette menu.

If you've included hyperlinks in an InDesign document, make sure you check Include Hyperlinks in the General panel of the Export Adobe PDF dialog box when you export the document as PDF. For information about exporting InDesign documents as PDF, see #95.

# #91 Creating Buttons

Adding hyperlinks is one way to add interactivity to InDesign documents that you export as PDF documents. Adding buttons is another. Buttons are similar to hyperlinks in that you can configure them to jump to other pages within the document, other documents, and URLs; however, buttons can also perform other actions, such as playing a movie or a sound, opening a file, or changing the view magnification.

To create a button:

1. Select the object you want to use as a button and choose Object > Interactive > Convert to Button.

2. With the object selected, choose Object > Interactive > Button Options. Use the controls in the General panel of the Button Options dialog box (**Figure 91**) to enter a name, add a description, and specify the button's visibility in the PDF.

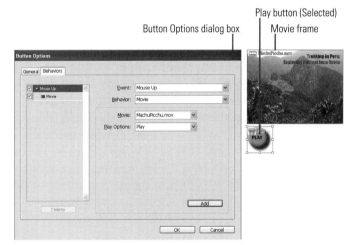

Button Options dialog box

Play button (Selected)

Movie frame

Figure 91 In this example, the Play button beneath the movie frame is configured to play when somebody clicks it (Event > Mouse Up). The controls in the Behaviors panel determine what happens when an Acrobat or Reader user interacts with the Play button.

*(continued on next page)*

## Button States

If you want to make a button in a PDF document look and behave more like a real-world button, you can configure it to display different graphics when a viewer moves the pointer over it or clicks it. The controls in the States palette (Window > Interactive > States) include three default button styles—Bevel, Drop Shadow, and Glow—or you can create custom styles. When you create a custom button style, you can assign a graphic or text to each of three mouse actions: Up (when the pointer is not over the button), Rollover (when the pointer is over the button), and Down (when a viewer clicks the button). You don't have to assign content for all three states. For example, you could configure a button that ignores a rollover and changes appearance only when a viewer clicks it.

3. Click Behaviors. The controls in the Behaviors panel let you specify what happens when the button is clicked in the PDF.

4. Choose a mouse action—Mouse Up, Mouse Down, Mouse Enter, or Mouse Exit—from the Event menu that will trigger the action. (The On Focus event lets you perform an action when a viewer of the PDF file presses the Tab key to select the button; the On Blur event lets you perform an action when a viewer presses Tab to select a different button or field.)

5. Choose an option from the Behavior menu. The action you choose in the Behavior menu determines the controls displayed. For example, if you choose Movie or Sound, you can select the movie or sound you want to play and specify play options. (See #92 for information about working with movies and sounds.)

6. Adjust the controls for the selected behavior. When you're done choosing settings, make sure you click Add to add the action to the scroll list.

7. When you finish specifying the behavior of the button, click OK.

If you want, you can add multiple mouse events with different behaviors, and you can add multiple behaviors to a single mouse event. For example, you could configure a single button that plays a sound when a PDF user moves the pointer within the button (Mouse Enter) and plays a movie when a viewer clicks the button (Mouse Up). Click Add each time you want to add Event/Behavior settings.

If you've included buttons in an InDesign document, make sure you check Include Interactive Elements in the General panel of the Export Adobe PDF dialog box when you export the document as PDF. For information about exporting InDesign documents as PDF, see #95.

# #92 Adding Movies and Sounds

The idea of adding movies and sounds to a layout may seem a bit strange, especially if you were around in the early days of page layout software. It wasn't that long ago that page layout programs let you create only printed publications. InDesign has expanded the boundaries by letting you create interactive multimedia PDF files that combine the best of print publishing—text and graphics—with rich media and hyperlinks.

Adding movies and sound files to a layout is much the same as adding graphics. The easiest method is to choose File > Place, and then select a movie or sound file. InDesign supports QuickTime, AVI, MPEG, and SWF movie files and AIF, AU, and WAV sound files. You can also drag and drop a movie or sound file from Windows Explorer or the Mac OS Finder into an InDesign layout.

To control how a movie file is handled when you export a layout as PDF and how the movie is displayed and plays in the exported PDF document, select a frame that contains a movie, and then choose Object > Interactive > Movie Options.

- The controls in the Source area of the Movie Options dialog box (**Figure 92a**) let you choose a movie file or specify a URL for a Web site that plays a streaming media file if an Internet connection is available.

- The controls in the Options area let you specify how the movie is displayed and how it plays in the PDF document.

- The Poster menu lets you choose the image that's displayed when the movie is not playing, and the Mode menu offers three choices for playing a movie: Play Once Then Stop, Play Once Stay Open, and Repeat Play.

## Working with Movies

You must have QuickTime 6 or later installed on your computer to work with movies in InDesign. If you don't have QuickTime 6, you can download it for free from Apple's Web site (www.apple.com).

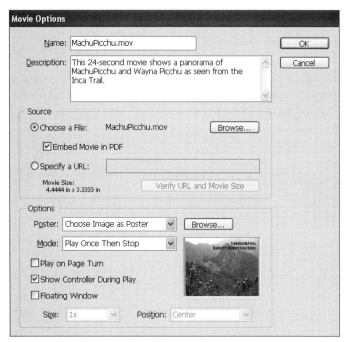

**Figure 92a** The Movie Options dialog box lets you specify a movie's source file and control how the movie is played when an Acrobat or Reader user views the PDF file.

To control how the sound file is handled when you export the layout as PDF and how the sound frame is displayed and plays in the exported PDF document, select a frame that contains a sound, and then choose Object > Interactive > Sound Options. The controls in the Sound Options dialog box (**Figure 92b**) are a subset of those in the Movie Options dialog box.

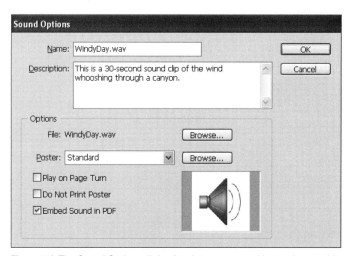

Figure 92b The Sound Options dialog box lets you control how a frame with a sound is displayed and how the sound file is handled when you export the layout as PDF.

**Viewing Multimedia PDF Documents**

If you intend to create multimedia PDF files with InDesign, keep in mind that Acrobat 6 or later is required to play MPEG and SWF movies in PDF documents. Acrobat 5 or later is required to play QuickTime and AVI movies.

When you export a layout that contains movies and sounds as PDF, you should export an Acrobat 6 (PDF 1.5) or Acrobat 7 (PDF 1.6) file, if possible. Acrobat 4 (PDF 1.3) and Acrobat 5 (PDF 1.4) files do not support all movie and sound features.

If you've included movies and sounds in an InDesign document, make sure you check Include Interactive Elements in the General panel of the Export Adobe PDF dialog box when you export the document as PDF. For information about exporting InDesign documents as PDF, see #95.

# CHAPTER ELEVEN

# Preflight and Output

As you work on a publication, you'll probably print several proofs to one or more desktop printers before the publication is completed. After you've added the final touches and the publication is ready for final output, you or your print service provider will print the finished document, probably using a high-resolution printer. If you're producing a color publication that will be printed on a printing press, *final output* means printing color separations that will be used to print the document on-press.

One of the main advantages of page layout software is that it lets you view publications onscreen before you print them. However, displaying a publication onscreen and printing it are very different processes. InDesign includes several features for troubleshooting potential printing problems before they occur, as well as an abundance of print-related controls that help ensure you get the results you want when you print a document.

In this chapter, you'll learn how to preview color separations onscreen, how to preflight a document before you print it to identify potential problems, and how to gather all the files required to print a document. You'll also learn how to export documents as PDF and use PDF presets to streamline PDF export, as well as how to export InDesign objects, pages, and documents for use in other InDesign documents and other media. Finally, you'll learn how to print documents and use print presets to save time and ensure consistent results.

# #93 Previewing Color Separations

InDesign includes several features that let you preview and prepare documents before you print final versions or send them to a print service provider for high-resolution output. The Separations Preview palette (Window > Output > Separations Preview) is one of the most useful production tools for color publications. It lets you show or hide individual colors, display color values for objects and graphics, and show areas that exceed a specified maximum ink coverage.

To preview color separations onscreen, open the Separations preview palette (**Figures 93a** and **93b**), and then choose Separations from the View menu. The color list in the palette includes process colors—cyan, magenta, yellow, and black, as well as any other spot colors in the Swatches palette regardless of whether you've used them.

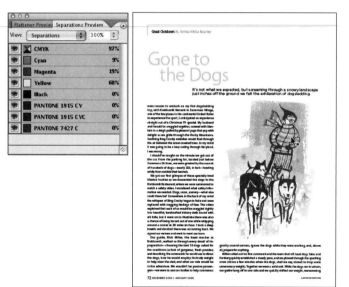

**Figure 93a** The Separations Preview palette includes a list of process and spot colors, and lets you show and hide individual colors. In this example, the pointer is on the sweater of the person in the graphic. The values in the palette show the color makeup of the pixel that the pointer is on.

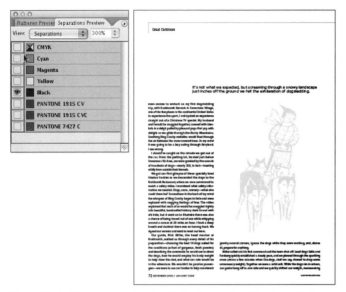

**Figure 93b** In this example, all colors in the Separations Preview palette are turned off except Black. Only objects that are black or contain a percentage of black are displayed on the document page.

## Preview Overprinting

To see an accurate onscreen representation of how objects that are set to overprint will look when printed, check Overprint Preview in the View menu. (Use the controls in the Attributes palette—Window > Attributes—to overprint an object's fill, stroke, or both.) Enabling Overprint Preview can slow down screen display, so you should use it only to check overprinted areas. Disable Overprint Preview when you return to working on a document.

Clicking the small square to the left of a color name alternately shows and hides the color. Clicking CMYK shows and hides all process colors. You can show or hide whatever colors you want, although at least one color must always be displayed. The Show Single Plates in Black command in the Separations Preview palette menu lets you control how a color is displayed when all other colors are hidden. When it's checked, single colors are displayed as black.

As you drag the pointer over a page, the values associated with the colors in the Separations Preview palette change to reflect the color of the pixel that the pointer is over.

**#93**: Previewing Color Separations

## Preview Display Mode

If you want to see how a document will look when it's printed, click the Preview button in the toolbox. The Preview display mode hides guidelines, gridlines, and objects that don't print, and displays a gray pasteboard. (Select an object, and then check Nonprinting in the Attributes palette to prevent it from printing.)

Because too much ink on a page can cause drying problems, you may also need to know if the colors in a layout exceed the maximum ink coverage value suggested by your print service provider. To highlight areas that exceed maximum ink coverage, choose Ink Limits in the palette menu, and then specify a maximum ink coverage value in the accompanying field. (Check with your print service provider for the suggested percentage.) Areas that exceed the specified maximum ink coverage value are displayed in shades of red. The more an area exceeds the maximum allowable ink coverage, the darker the shade of red.

When you're done previewing separations and areas that exceed maximum ink coverage, choose Off from the Separations Preview palette menu to return to normal view.

# #94 Preflighting and Packaging Documents

When it's time to send a finished InDesign document to a print service provider, there's still quite a bit of file management work that needs to be done: You need to gather all of the font and graphic files used in the document, as well as a copy of the InDesign file, into a single folder for easy transport. Fortunately, InDesign can do this file management work for you.

In addition to collecting font and graphic files, the Package command (File menu) scans a document for potential printing problems—a process called *preflight,* a term that's borrowed from the aviation industry—and warns you if it finds anything amiss. (You can also preflight a document without collecting font and graphic files by choosing File > Preflight.)

To preflight and package a document:

1. Choose File > Package. You'll be prompted to save the document if you've made changes since you last saved it.

2. If the preflight check does not find any potential problems, the Printing Instructions dialog box is displayed. If problems are found, an alert is displayed. If you click View Info in the alert, the Preflight dialog box is displayed (**Figure 94a**) and the problems are summarized in the Summary panel. The other panels display details. If you click Continue, the Printing Instructions dialog box is displayed.

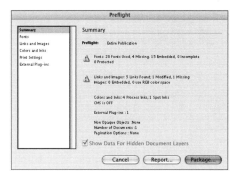

**Figure 94a**
The Preflight dialog box displays information about potential printing problems. In this example, the Summary panel indicates that four fonts are missing, one graphic has been modified, and one graphic is missing.

*(continued on next page)*

**Preflighting and Packaging Books**

To preflight or package a book, choose File > Open to open the book file. Then choose Preflight Book or Package > Book for Print from the Book palette menu.

3. The information you enter into the various fields of the Printing Instructions dialog box is saved as a text file that's included in the package. After you've entered the information you want to include, click Continue.

4. In the Create Package Folder dialog box (**Figure 94b**), enter a name for the folder into which files will be copied and specify its location.

5. Use the check boxes at the bottom of the dialog box to specify the files you want to include. You'll probably want to check Copy Fonts (Except CJK) and Copy Linked Graphics, and you should check Update Graphic Links in Package so that the InDesign file that's copied into the package folder is linked to the graphic files that are copied to the package folder and not the originals. (Linked graphics are placed within a folder called Links within the Package folder; fonts are placed within a folder called Fonts.)

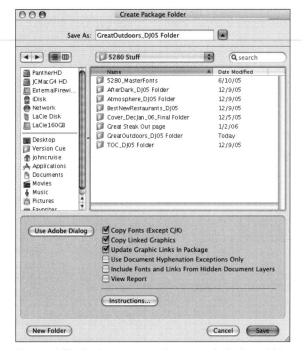

**Figure 94b** The Package command creates a folder into which the files you specify in the Create Package Folder dialog box are copied. Send the package folder to your print service provider for final output.

# #95 Exporting Documents as PDF

At many publishing sites, publications in progress are exported as PDF documents for electronic markup and review, and finished publications are exported as PDF for final, high-resolution output. When it's time to export an InDesign layout as a PDF file, you have many options for controlling the size and many other characteristics of the file. The choices you make when you export a PDF file depend on how the PDF will be used. For example, if you want to distribute a PDF via email to colleagues or clients for electronic review and markup using Acrobat or Reader, you should save a compact, low-resolution PDF that's ideal for electronic distribution and review but not appropriate for high-resolution output. If you intend to send a PDF file to a print service provider for high-resolution output, you should save a high-resolution file.

To export a layout as PDF:

1. Choose File > Export.

2. In the Export dialog box, enter a name for the PDF file and choose the folder in which the file will be saved.

3. Choose Adobe PDF from the Format menu (Mac OS) or Save as Type menu (Windows), and then click Save.

4. At this point, you can simply choose a PDF preset in the Adobe PDF Preset menu, and then click Export, or you can choose a preset, customize the settings in the various panels of the Export Adobe PDF dialog box (**Figure 95**), and then click Export. (For more about using PDF presets, see #96.) If you change a setting, "(modified)" is displayed to the right of the preset selected in the Adobe PDF Preset menu.

## Exporting Books

If you've used InDesign's book feature to combine several layouts into a book, you can export all documents or selected documents as PDF. (For more about books, see #85.) To export all documents in a book as a single PDF file, open the book file, click a blank area in the Book palette, and then choose Export Book to PDF. To export some but not all documents, select the documents you want to export in the Book palette, and then choose Export Selected Documents to PDF. The rest of the process is the same as exporting a document as PDF.

## Exporting Interactive, Multimedia PDFs

When you export a PDF document that contains bookmarks, hyperlinks, buttons, and multimedia files (pictures and sounds), make sure you check Bookmarks, Hyperlinks, and Interactive Elements in the General panel of the Export Adobe PDF dialog box.

## Copying Objects as PDF

You can also use PDF to copy objects from InDesign to PDF-aware programs like Illustrator and Photoshop. For example, if you've created a graphic in InDesign and you want to use it in a Photoshop image, you can copy the object in InDesign and then paste it into Photoshop. If you check Copy PDF to Clipboard in the File Handling panel of the InDesign Preferences dialog box, PDF data is copied to the clipboard when you choose Edit > Copy or Edit > Cut. To use copied objects in a PDF-aware program, switch to that program, and then choose Edit > Paste.

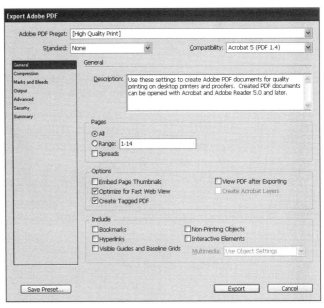

**Figure 95** When you export an InDesign document as PDF, the settings you make in the panels of the Export Adobe PDF dialog box determine the size and characteristics of the PDF document.

When you make changes in the Export Adobe PDF dialog box, they're saved with the application and used the next time you export a layout as PDF.

# #96 Using PDF Presets

A PDF preset is a predefined collection of PDF export settings that balances file size and resolution to produce a PDF file that's appropriate for a particular use, such as high-resolution output or onscreen display and review. When you install InDesign, five default PDF presets are included. Here's a brief description of each:

- **Smallest File Size:** Produces PDFs that are suitable for electronic distribution and onscreen display. This preset is not appropriate for high-resolution printing.

- **High Quality Print:** Produces PDFs that are suitable for printing proofs to laser and inkjet printers.

- **Press Quality:** Produces PDFs that are suitable for high-resolution output.

- **PDF/X-1a 2001:** Creates a PDF file that conforms to the PDF/X-1a standard that is commonly used for ads provided to print publications.

- **PDF/X-3 2002:** Creates a PDF file that conforms to the PDF/X-3 standard, which is similar to PDF/X-1a.

When you export an InDesign layout as PDF, you must choose a PDF preset in the Export Adobe PDF dialog box. You can either use the default settings of the selected PDF preset as is, or you can modify them, and you can save modified settings as a custom PDF preset.

To save a custom PDF preset, modify the settings in the Export Adobe PDF dialog box, and then click Save Preset. Assign a name in the Save Preset dialog box. After you save a PDF preset, it's displayed in the Adobe PDF Preset menu in the Export Adobe PDF dialog box, along with the five default presets and any other presets you've created or received from your print service provider.

## Sharing PDF Presets

The Save As button in the Adobe PDF Presets dialog box lets you save a PDF preset as a .joboptions file that you can share with other InDesign users. PDF presets are stored in a specific folder that InDesign (and other Adobe Creative Suite applications) accesses when it displays a list of available presets (for example, in the Adobe PDF Presets dialog box). On a Macintosh computer, the file path to the PDF presets folder is \Library\Application Support\ Adobe PDF\Settings. On a Windows computer, the file path is *<default drive>*:\Documents and Settings\All Users\Documents\ Adobe PDF\Setting. You can drag .joboptions files to the PDF folder, or you can simply double-click a .joboptions file to automatically move it to the correct folder. You can also use the Load button in the Adobe PDF Presets dialog box to move a .joboptions file to the folder that contains PDF presets.

You can also create a custom PDF preset by choosing File > Adobe PDF Presets > Define. The Adobe PDF Presets dialog box (**Figure 96**) displays a list of currently available presets. Click New to create a new preset, or select a preset in the list and click Edit to modify it.

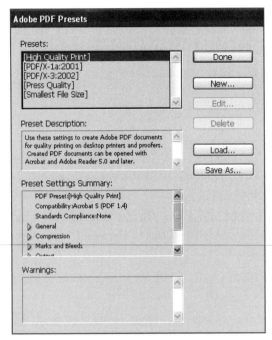

**Figure 96** The Adobe PDF Presets dialog box displays a list of available PDF presets, and includes controls for adding new presets, editing and deleting existing presets, and loading and saving PDF preset (.joboptions) files.

# #97 Exporting Documents in Other Formats

Sometimes, you may want to use an InDesign page in another application or in another InDesign document. For example, if you've created a magazine cover, you may want to use a reduced version of the page in an advertisement for the magazine. Or you may want to include an image of the cover on a Web page. Similarly, you may want to use the text in an InDesign document in a different program. InDesign lets you export objects, text, pages, spreads, and documents in a variety of different file formats.

To export an object or multiple objects, text, or document pages, choose File > Export. The Export dialog box is displayed (**Figure 97**). The file formats displayed in the Format menu and what you can export depends on what's currently selected in the document: nothing, one or more objects, a text frame, or text.

**Figure 97** When a text frame is selected or text is highlighted, the Format menu in the Export dialog box includes text file formats, such as Rich Text Format and Text Only, as well as graphic formats, such as EPS and JPEG.

The Format menu in the Export dialog box offers the following choices:

- **Adobe InDesign Tagged Text:** This text file format saves all InDesign text-formatting codes. If you open a tagged text file in a word processing program, the formatting codes are displayed along with the text. If you import a tagged text file into InDesign, the formatting codes are applied to the text and are not visible. This option is available only if a text frame is selected or text is highlighted.

- **Adobe PDF:** This option lets you export a page, multiple pages, or a document as PDF. See #95 for more information about exporting documents as PDF.

- **EPS:** If you need to use an InDesign page in another program or another InDesign document, the EPS file format is the best option. When you export as EPS, you can export a page, a spread, a range or pages, or all pages. Each page or spread is saved as a separate EPS file.

- **InDesign Interchange:** If you, a colleague, or a client needs to open an InDesign CS2 document using InDesign CS, you can export the InDesign CS2 document using the InDesign Interchange format. If any objects use features that are new in InDesign CS2, they may be modified or omitted when the file is opened in InDesign CS.

- **JPEG:** The JPEG file format is often used for images in Web pages. When you export as JPEG, you can export an object, a page, a spread, a range of pages, or all pages. Each page or spread is saved as a separate JPEG file.

- **Rich Text Format:** The Rich Text Format (RTF) converts all text formatting to text instructions that other programs, particularly Microsoft Word, can recognize. Not all of the text-formatting features in InDesign are supported by RTF. For example, horizontal/vertical scaling, optical kerning, and shear are not supported. This option is available only if a text frame is selected or text is highlighted.

- **SVG:** The Scalable Vector Graphics format can be used to create Web pages with high-resolution graphics that include data. When you export as SVG, you can export an object, a page, a spread, a range of pages, or all pages.

- **SVG Compressed:** This is a compressed version of the SVG file format.

- **Text Only:** This option saves a .txt file and removes all paragraph and character formatting. This option is available only if a text frame is selected or text is highlighted.

- **XML:** Similar to HTML files, XML files include tags that describe text and graphic content, but do not include information about how the content is displayed or formatted. The XML file format is particularly useful for using the same content across different media. Before you can export a document as XML, you must assign XML tags to the document's objects.

# #**98** Printing Documents

## Printing a Book

To print a book, choose File > Open and open the book file. Then choose Print Book from the Book palette menu. The Print dialog box is displayed.

While you can use InDesign to produce nonprinted documents, such as interactive multimedia PDFs, chances are you'll print most of the documents you create. Whether you need to print proofs of a layout you're working on to an inkjet or laser printer or send a finished layout to a high-resolution printer, such as an imagesetter, you can use InDesign's extensive printing controls to ensure that you get the results you want.

Before you print a document, it's a good idea to preflight it (File > Preflight; see #94) to determine whether there are any potential printing problems and, if so, fix them. You should also make sure that the correct drivers and PostScript Printer Descriptions (PPDs) are installed on your computer. When you're ready to print, choose File > Print.

To specify the printer, choose a print preset from the Print Preset menu in the Print dialog box (**Figure 98**), or choose Custom if you want to modify settings in any of the Print dialog box panels. (For more about print presets, see #100.) You can also choose a printer from the Printer menu.

If you choose a print preset, all you have to do is click Print. All of the settings in the General, Setup, Marks and Bleeds, Output, Graphics, Color Management, and Advanced panels of the Print dialog box are automatically set based on the settings in the selected preset. You can specify custom print settings by making changes in any of the panels. When you modify default settings for a print preset or choose a different printer from the Printer list, "[Custom]" is displayed in the Print Preset menu.

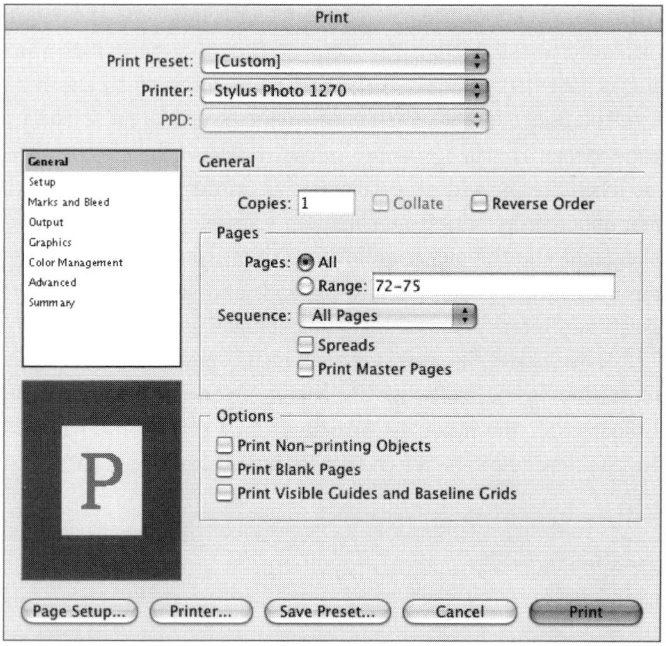

**Figure 98** The Print dialog box contains several panels of controls for specifying printing settings. Here you see the General panel, which lets you choose a printer, specify the pages to print, and provides options for printing objects, blank pages, and guidelines and gridlines that wouldn't otherwise print.

The print dialog box contains several dozen controls—too many to attempt to explain here. It's a good idea to examine the controls in each panel so that you know what's available. You probably won't need to change many of the controls very often, but if you do, familiarity will come in handy.

**Printing Transparency**

When you print a document that includes transparency effects, such as soft drop shadows, InDesign performs a process called *flattening* before it sends transparent objects to the printer. During flattening, areas where transparent objects overlap other objects are either rasterized or converted into vector data that the printer can understand. Flattening doesn't affect objects on pages; only the information that's sent to the printer. If you send your InDesign documents, or exported PDF versions of your documents, to a print service provider, it's a good idea to let the provider know if your documents contain transparency.

**Sending PDF Files to a Print Service Provider**

Some print service providers prefer to receive PDF files rather than native InDesign files. If that's the case, you'll need to save the document as PDF before sending it to your provider. (For more information about exporting PDFs, see #95.)

# #99 Creating Printer Spreads

When you create multipage documents with InDesign, the pages are displayed in the document window in the same order that a reader would read them. Page 1 is the first page, followed by pages 2 and 3 (displayed together), then pages 4 and 5, and so on. Each facing-page spread is called a *reader spread*. However, before a multipage document is printed at a commercial printer, the pages must be rearranged into printer spreads. For example, the first page of a document and the last page form a printer spread. Pages 2 and the next-to-last page are a printer spread, and so on. The process of creating printer spreads from reader spreads is called *imposition*.

The InBooklet SE command (File menu) provides several controls for specifying how multipage documents are printed. When you choose InBooklet SE, the InBooklet SE dialog box is displayed (**Figure 99a**). The Style menu offers five choices for imposing a document:

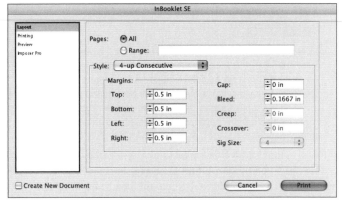

**Figure 99a** The Layout panel in the InBooklet SE dialog box lets you control how multipage documents are printed. The Style menu provides five imposition options. The controls available in the dialog box depend on the option you select in the Style menu.

- **2-up Saddle Stitch:** This option creates two-page, side-by-side printer spreads. When you choose this option, the InBooklet SE dialog box displays options for controlling Margins, Bleed, and Creep.

- **2-up Perfect Bound:** This option is similar to 2-up Saddle Stitch but also includes controls for Gap, Crossover, and Signature Size.

- **2-up Consecutive, 3-up Consecutive, and 4-up Consecutive:** All of these options create multipage panels that are appropriate for a foldout publication or a brochure. Margin controls as well as Gap and Bleed controls are available if you choose any of these options.

Here's a brief description of the controls in the InBooklet SE dialog box:

- **Margins:** The values you enter in the Margins area determine the amount of space that surrounds a printer spread after it is trimmed.

- **Gap:** The amount of space between adjacent pages.

- **Bleed:** The distance beyond the edge of the page that is printed. Objects that extend beyond the edge are printed up to the specified bleed distance.

- **Creep:** The Creep value you enter accommodates for the accumulated thickness of the paper and folding.

- **Crossover:** This determines the distance within the specified Gap that objects extending beyond the inner edge of a page will print (somewhat like a bleed for the inner edges of a spread).

- **Sig(nature) Size:** This specifies the number of pages in a perfect bound document and is available only if you choose 2-up Perfect Bound from the Style menu.

If you check Create New Document in the InBooklet SE dialog box, InBooklet SE creates a new document using the specified settings when you click Print. If you don't check Create New Document, InBooklet SE rearranges the pages of the document.

The controls in the Printing panel are similar to the controls available in the Marks and Bleed panel of InDesign's Print dialog box. For example, you can add crop marks, registration marks, bleed marks, gray bars, and color bars, as well as custom information.

The Preview panel (**Figure 99b**) displays a preview of how the document will print using the settings you've specified in the Layout and Printing panels.

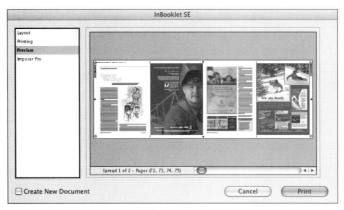

**Figure 99b** The Preview panel of the InBooklet SE dialog box shows how a document will print based on the settings specified in the Layout and Printing panels.

# #**100** Using Print Presets

Most publishing sites have multiple printers, and they're used for different purposes. For example, writers and editors often use black-and-white laser printers to output hard copies for manual editing, whereas designers often use color inkjet or color laser printers to output color proofs. If you send your InDesign documents to multiple printers, using print presets can save time and help ensure consistent results.

Print presets are similar to PDF presets. (For more about PDF presets, see #96.) A print preset is a saved collection of print settings that lets you quickly print a document to a specific printer without having to manually specify settings in the Print dialog box.

The easiest way to create a print preset is to use the Print dialog box (File > Print). Choose an output device from the Printer menu, choose a PostScript printer description from the PPD menu, and then select the appropriate settings in the various panels of the Print dialog box. When you're finished specifying settings, click Save Preset, and then name the preset. After you save a preset, its name is displayed in the Print dialog box's Print Preset menu, and you can choose it whenever you need to print a document to the specified printer.

In addition to printing a file by choosing File > Print, and then choosing a print preset, you can also choose File > Print Preset, and then choose a print preset from the submenu. The Print dialog box is displayed, and the print preset you chose is selected in the Print Preset menu.

You can also create print presets by choosing File > Print Preset > Define, and then clicking New in the Print Presets dialog box (**Figure 100**). This displays the New Print Preset dialog box, which is identical to the Print dialog box. The Print Presets dialog box also includes buttons that let you edit or delete existing print presets, as well as buttons for saving a print preset file and for loading a saved preset file. The ability to save and load print preset files enables you to share print presets with colleagues, clients, and print service providers.

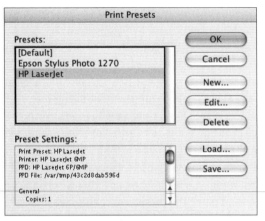

**Figure 100** The Print Presets dialog box displays a list of available print presets and includes buttons for adding new presets, editing and deleting existing presets, and saving and loading presets.

# Index